WRITERS OF THE HOLOCAUST

GLOBAL PROFILES

WRITERS OF THE HOLOCAUST

Sherri Lederman Mandell

✓® Facts On File, Inc.

Writers of the Holocaust

Copyright © 1999 by Sherri Lederman Mandell

Illustrations on pages x, xii–xiii, xv, and xix copyright © 1999 Facts On File

Facts On File, Inc.
11 Penn Plaza
New York NY 10001

Library of Congress Cataloging-in-Publication Data
Mandell, Sherri Lederman.
    Writers of the Holocaust / Sherri Lederman Mandell.
        p.   cm.—(Global profiles)
    Summary: Profiles ten men and women who have written about or whose writings were influenced by their experiences during the Holocaust.
    ISBN 0-8160-3729-9
    1. Holocaust, Jewish (1939–1945)—Personal narratives—History and criticism—Juvenile literature. 2. Holocaust, Jewish (1939–1945), in literature—Juvenile literature. 3. Jewish authors—Biography—Juvenile literature. [1. Holocaust, Jewish (1939–1945)—Personal narratives. 2. Jews—Biography.] I. Title. II. Series.
D804.195.M36   1999
940.53′18′0922—dc 21
                                                                    98-23601

Facts On File books are available at special discounts when purchased in bulk quantities for businesses, associations, institutions or sales promotions. Please call our Special Sales Department in New York at (212) 967-8800 or (800) 322-8755.

You can find Facts On File on the World Wide Web at http://www.factsonfile.com

Text design by Cathy Rincon
Cover design by Nora Wertz
Illustrations on pages x, xii–xiii, xv, and xix by Jeremy Eagle

Printed in the United States of America

MP FOF 10 9 8 7 6 5 4 3 2 1

This book is printed on acid-free paper.

In memory of my father,

Paul Lederman

1922–1997

Contents

Acknowledgments

I am grateful to Aharon Appelfeld, Ida Fink, Shirley Kaufman, and Vitka Kovner for their gracious conversation and their generous help with this book. I want to thank Andrea Peskoff and Aryeh Breslov for commenting on the manuscript, Jan Engoren for helping with research, and Anne Breslov for her support. Thanks to my sister Nancy Lederman for encouraging me, and to my sister Loren Fogelson and my mother, Marilyn Lederman, for their research work. I also want to mention my mother-in-law, Lillian Mandell, and my children, Koby, Daniel, Eliana, and Gavriel, whose joy and energy sustained me while writing this book. Finally, I want to thank my husband, Seth—faithful reader and friend.

Birthplaces*

1 Yitzhak Katznelson
2 Abba Kovner
3 Primo Levi
4 Hannah Senesh
5 Ida Fink

6 Arnošt Lustig
7 Elie Wiesel
8 Anne Frank
9 Aharon Appelfeld
10 Jerzy Kosinski

○ Place of birth
✹ Capital city of country of birth

* Current political boundaries are shown for reference. In some cases, subject's "country of birth" has changed along with political boundaries.

Introduction

This book profiles the lives and literary contributions of 10 men and women who were victims of the Holocaust. Each person wrote about his or her experiences during World War II. It is through their diaries, memoirs, novels, short stories, and poetry that the terrible evil that was unleashed during the Holocaust is most powerfully conveyed.

The word *Holocaust* means great or terrible destruction. The "great and terrible destruction" refers to the persecution and killing of more than 6 million Jews by Nazi Germany and its collaborators between the years of 1933 and 1945. However, Adolf Hitler, the German leader who came to power in 1933, did not reserve his hatred only for Jews. Hundreds of thousands of Catholics, Poles, Gypsies, Jehovah's Witnesses, homosexuals, and handicapped people were also persecuted and killed by Hitler's forces.

Hitler began the war to restore and expand Germany's power. He also waged a separate war to purify the German race. Hitler blamed Jews for Germany's defeat in World War I and the country's subsequent economic depression. He believed that people with German or Aryan (northern European) backgrounds were superior and that other races threatened the purity of the German race. In particular, he targeted

The Nazis created hundreds of camps where they imprisoned and murdered
larger of these camps and most of those mentioned in this book.

AND THE NAZI-OCCUPIED TERRITORIES

Jews, Gypsies, political enemies, and other victims. This map includes the

Jews (who were less than 1 percent of the German population in 1933) to be eliminated from German society.

Harsh anti-Jewish measures followed Hitler's election as chancellor on January 30, 1933. On April 1, 1933, the Nazis, members of Hitler's National Socialist German Workers Party, organized a nationwide boycott of Jewish-owned businesses. In 1935, laws passed in Nuremberg made anti-Semitism official German government policy. Jews had their citizenship revoked and were forbidden from marrying non-Jews. They could no longer vote or work in government offices. Other laws stipulated that anyone with one Jewish grandparent was considered Jewish, regardless of the religion they practiced. By 1938, Jews were segregated politically, economically, and socially. Jewish children were forbidden from school.

Many Jews fled the country; those who didn't were persecuted and terrorized. On November 9, 1938, there was an

Destruction of a Jewish synagogue in Siegen, Germany, during Kristallnacht, November 9, 1938 (Yad VaShem)

GHETTOS IN OCCUPIED EASTERN EUROPE, 1941–1942

Between 1939 and 1943, the Germans forced hundreds of thousands of Jews into more than 400 ghettos.

organized riot, called Kristallnacht (Night of Broken Glass), directed against Jews in Germany and Austria. Nazis destroyed synagogues, businesses, and homes and murdered Jews. Some 30,000 Jews were sent to concentration camps. Ninety-one Jews were killed.

World War II officially began on September 1, 1939, when Germany invaded Poland. By the summer of 1940, Hitler was making his dream of world domination a reality. He had conquered most of western and eastern Europe, including Austria, Denmark, Norway, France, and the Netherlands. The Nazis occupied Greece, Syria, and North Africa. They were invading Russia and planning the takeover of England and Ireland.

When the Nazis invaded a country, Nazi persecution of the Jews followed a similar pattern. In each country, the Nazis had help from some of the local population in terrorizing the Jews. The Nazis and their collaborators forced the Jews to wear a yellow star of identification. Jews were forbidden to do business, to travel, and to shop except at certain stores. They were confined to their homes in the evenings. Their belongings and property, including businesses, money, and jewels, were confiscated.

In 1940, the Nazis began to enclose the Jews in ghettos, sealed areas where the Jews were forced to live, cut off from the rest of the population. Jews suffered from starvation and diseases such as typhoid and typhus in these ghettos. Many were also forced to do slave labor for the Nazis. Then in late 1941 and in 1942, the Germans began to destroy the ghettos. After a meeting of top German government leaders in January 1942 at the Wannsee Convention in a Berlin suburb, the Nazis formalized the "Final Solution," the planned annihilation of the Jewish people. Already in Russia, special killing squads were gunning down Jews, massacring whole villages.

Women and children on their way to the gas chambers in Auschwitz, June 1944 (Yad VaShem)

The Nazis told the Jews of Poland and eastern Europe that they were being "resettled"—sent from the ghettos to work camps. Many Jews hoped that their conditions would improve. Instead the unimaginable occurred: Most Jews were deported to death camps where they were killed by poison gas. Their bodies were then burned in furnaces.

In Belzec, Sobibor, Chełmno, Majdanek, Auschwitz-Birkenau, and Treblinka, Jews met their death in gas chambers and furnaces at the rate of 10,000 a day. Through a selection process, some Jews were chosen to labor in work and death camps, assisting in the German war effort. Only these Jews were allowed to live. In some cases, these survivors were forced to run the death chambers, at times forced to see their loved ones die in front of them.

Sometimes students today wonder why the Jews didn't fight back. The answer is complex. The Jews did not know or believe that the Nazis intended to exterminate them. The Jews felt that they could survive the war in the face of restrictions and persecution. In addition, Jews who did fight back risked their families' lives because the Germans threatened severe reprisals, including collective punishment. If one Jew revolted, as many as 150 Jews were shot. Most Jews believed that the important thing was to stay together with their families and endure the hardships they faced.

And when they did fight back, like some of the writers profiled in this book (for example, Abba Kovner, Yitzhak Katznelson, and Hannah Senesh), they were soon overwhelmed by the superior firepower of the Nazi forces. It must be remembered that the Jews lacked an army, and the arms they did occasionally have were meager.

Still in every ghetto and concentration camp, there were those who resisted. In fact, during the Warsaw ghetto rebellion, the Jews battled the German army for almost a month—longer than the Polish army had resisted. In addition, about 20,000 to 30,000 Jews fought in resistance groups based in the forests of eastern Europe. But resistance was difficult and dangerous, and the possibility of success was limited.

On June 6, 1944, or D day, the armies opposing Hitler—the Allies, including the Americans, the Russians, and the British—invaded western Europe. Although the Nazis had invaded more than 20 countries, the Allies finally succeeded in stopping the Nazi war machine. Before Germany surrendered on May 7, 1945, Hitler killed himself. In Europe, between 30 and 35 million soldiers and civilians were dead, including 6 million Jews. Two out of every three European

Jews had been murdered, including a million and a half Jewish children.

The Holocaust was a time of unimaginable evil. It was a time of unprecedented cruelty: mothers forced to watch their children killed; people forced to dig their own graves before being shot and thrown in them.

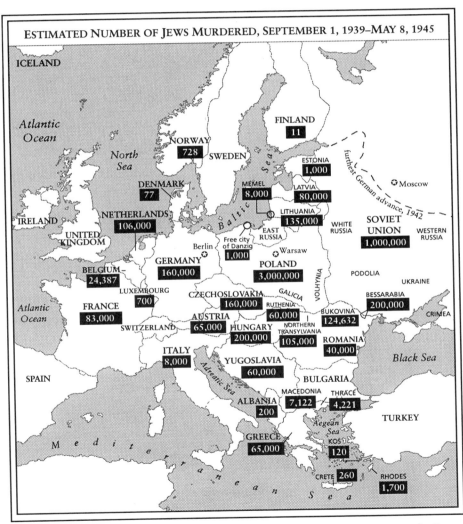

ESTIMATED NUMBER OF JEWS MURDERED, SEPTEMBER 1, 1939–MAY 8, 1945

ICELAND

Atlantic Ocean

FINLAND
11

NORWAY
728

North Sea

SWEDEN

ESTONIA
1,000

◇ Moscow

furthest German advance, 1942

DENMARK
77

MEMEL
8,000

LATVIA
80,000

IRELAND

NETHERLANDS
106,000

LITHUANIA
135,000

WHITE RUSSIA

SOVIET UNION
1,000,000

WESTERN RUSSIA

UNITED KINGDOM

Berlin

EAST RUSSIA

Free city of Danzig
1,000

Berlin ◇

◇ Warsaw

GERMANY
160,000

POLAND
3,000,000

PODOLIA

UKRAINE

BELGIUM–
24,387

LUXEMBOURG
700

CZECHOSLOVAKIA
160,000

GALICIA

VOLHYNIA

RUTHENIA

BESSARABIA
200,000

Atlantic Ocean

FRANCE
83,000

SWITZERLAND

AUSTRIA
65,000

HUNGARY
200,000

NORTHERN TRANSYLVANIA
105,000

BUKOVINA
124,632

ROMANIA
40,000

CRIMEA

ITALY
8,000

Adriatic Sea

YUGOSLAVIA
60,000

BULGARIA

Black Sea

SPAIN

MACEDONIA
7,122

THRACE
4,221

ALBANIA
200

Aegean Sea

TURKEY

M e d i t e r r a n e a n   S e a

GREECE
65,000

KOS
120

CRETE **260**

RHODES
1,700

Two-thirds of the Jews in Europe were killed during the Holocaust, including 1.5 million children.

One of the best ways to remember and bear witness to that atrocity is through literature. Aharon Appelfeld, an Israeli novelist, was only nine when he escaped from a concentration camp, alone, to wander through the Ukrainian countryside for three years. He insists that it is important to remember that each person who was killed has a story, his or her own unique story: parents, brothers and sisters, teachers, friends, dreams, and loves. Literature is also, perhaps, the best way to tell each person's story. Appelfeld's goal in his writing is to give back to each person who died his or her particular name, his or her family—his or her individuality.

Writers who write about the Holocaust pay tribute to those who died. They also show the strength of the human spirit. To emerge from catastrophe and still want to give voice, to bear witness, is an affirmation of humanity.

Writing is a desire to communicate, a desire to say this happened, these people were important, and it is important that we remember them.

Elie Wiesel, the Nobel prize–winning author and humanitarian, has said that he believes testimony is the most powerful tool we have for remembering the Holocaust. Testimony is an eyewitness report, primary evidence. Testimony is powerful because it brings the reader or listener close to what the victim experienced.

In this book of profiles, testimony takes the form of diaries, memoirs, novels, short stories, and poems. Diaries are written close to the time of the actual events, while memoirs are writers' memories of what happened, written at a later time. Fiction in its various forms, of course, is by definition imaginary literature, an invented story, but it can be based on fact and in some cases can present the truth in sharper focus. Appelfeld says he needed to transform his experience into fiction because if he had written exactly what had happened to him, nobody would have believed it. He adds that now, looking back after 50 years, it is difficult even for him to believe that what he experienced could have happened. The horror is that incomprehensible. That is not to say the events did not occur. They did. But they are so repugnant, so evil, so brutal, so unreal, that they defy understanding.

Literature is a search for meaning. But what happened during the Holocaust, the terrible cruelty and suffering, cannot be given meaning, so the writer is left with the dilemma of giving voice to a situation that defies meaning, that defies reconciliation.

Some of the writers profiled in this book were children during the war, others adults. Some survived the war; others were killed. Many saw their entire family and village destroyed. The writers are from different countries: Poland, Italy, Hungary, Holland, Bukovina (now a region in Romania and Ukraine), and Czechoslovakia. They write in different languages. Each author profiled in this book gives us a different view, a different angle, of the same catastrophe in history.

Yitzhak Katznelson, the first writer presented, is a father who saw his children and wife destroyed, sent to concentration camps from the Warsaw ghetto. He wrote a diary and a long poem, *Song of the Murdered Jewish People*, before he himself was sent to Auschwitz. He is a father who suffers, the father of not just his own family but of the whole family of Jewish people.

Abba Kovner survived the war as a partisan, a resistance fighter. He banded with others, living in the Lithuanian forest and fighting the Nazis. His book-length poem *My Little Sister* gives voice to his people's suffering and his guilt at not being able to save them.

Primo Levi was an Italian chemist who became a writer. His work, especially his memoir of life in Auschwitz, *Survival in Auschwitz*, is heartbreaking in its close observation of the details of the concentration camp and the people in them.

Hannah Senesh was an idealistic young woman who left Palestine (which in 1948 was divided into Israel and the western portion of Jordan) and parachuted into Europe in 1944 in order to return to her native country of Hungary and try to save her mother and people. Her diary and poems show us the picture of a young woman brimming with love and enthusiasm.

Ida Fink, who is from Poland, lived in hiding during the war and writes about the way ordinary life intermingled with the brutality of the war. Her book *A Scrap of Time*, a series of short stories, shows us the way that the most ordinary events, even time itself, took on a different meaning because of the war.

Arnošt Lustig, who is from Czechoslovakia but is currently living in the United States, survived three concentration camps. In his numerous novels and short stories, he confronts questions of ethics and declares that to survive the Holocaust was not enough. People had to survive with a clean conscience, even if they had to die for their adherence to moral standards. He insists that heroism and courage were not only possible but necessary responses to the evil that befell the Jews.

Elie Wiesel, from Hungary, is a witness compelled to speak. As a 16-year-old boy, he witnessed his father's death in a concentration camp. A deeply religious boy, Wiesel, as a man, struggled to maintain his faith in God. In all of his writing, he continues to question: Where was God during the Holocaust? And even more poignantly: Where was man? Wiesel believes in the truth of silence but is forced to speak, to remember the dead, to make sure that their death is not forgotten. His book *Night* is a masterpiece at conveying the nightmare confronted by victims during the Holocaust.

In her diary Anne Frank, who lived in Holland, presents a picture of a girl who was a model of courage. She wrote about what it was like to be a teenager living in hiding under extraordinary circumstances. Her diary is all the more heartbreaking because the reader knows the horrible fate that awaits her. She died in Bergen-Belsen concentration camp in 1944.

Aharon Appelfeld was born in Bukovina and lives in Israel. An author of novels and short stories, he writes about people who are oppressed by what they experienced during the Holocaust, who are no longer whole, but who endure, forever seeking the home that has been taken from them.

Writer Jerzy Kosinski was born in Poland and later moved to the United States. In his work, he forces us to confront evil. His book *The Painted Bird* depicts a series of horrifying episodes in which the reader is confronted with brutality—and is perhaps the most brutal book written about the Holocaust.

The Holocaust killed not just people but people's belief in humanity. These writers retrieve our belief in humanity. They were all victims, but they are also all heroes. They insist that we remember. And by writing and remembering, the writers try to make sure that such a terrible event will never happen again.

Chronology

January 30, 1933	Adolf Hitler becomes chancellor of Germany
September 15, 1935	Nuremberg Laws decree that German citizenship belongs only to those "of German or related blood"; marriage between Jews and Germans is prohibited
March 13, 1938	Germany annexes Austria
November 9–10	Kristallnacht: In Germany and Austria, synagogues are burned and Jewish businesses looted; Jewish men are deported to concentration camps
September 1, 1939	Germany invades Poland; World War II begins
Spring 1940	Germany invades and defeats Denmark, Norway, Belgium, Luxembourg, the Netherlands, and France
October	Jews of Warsaw are sealed in a ghetto
June 22, 1941	Germans invade the Soviet Union; mass killings of Jews, Gypsies, and Communist leaders take place
December 7	Japan attacks Pearl Harbor
December 8	first gassing of Jews at Chełmno extermination camp in Poland occurs
December 11	United States declares war on Germany and Italy
1942	mass murder of Jews begins at Auschwitz, Treblinka, Sobibor, Belzec, and Majdanek death camps
April 19–May 16, 1943	Warsaw ghetto uprising
March 19, 1944	Germany occupies Hungary
June 6	D day: Allies invade western Europe

January 17, 1945	Nazis evacuate Auschwitz; prisoners be-gin forced death marches
January 27	Soviet troops liberate Auschwitz
May 7, 1945	Germany surrenders and the war ends in Europe

WRITERS
OF THE
HOLOCAUST

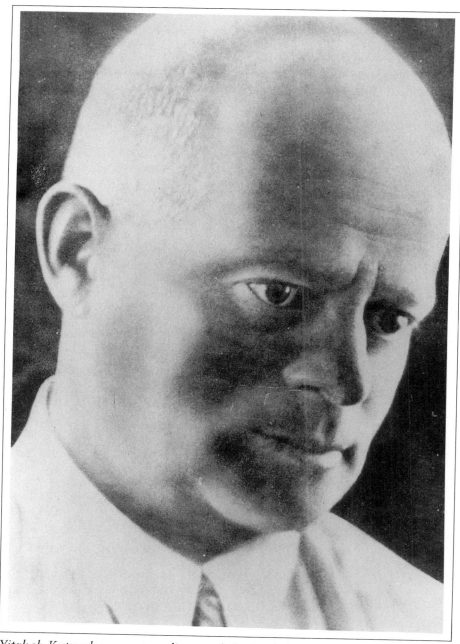

Yitzhak Katznelson wrote a diary and the book-length poem The Song of
the Murdered Jewish People *before he was killed in Auschwitz.*
(Yad VaShem)

Yitzhak Katznelson

(1886–1944)

Yitzhak Katznelson sat in darkness on the cellar floor, hiding from the Nazis. It was September 4, 1942, and Katznelson was in the Warsaw ghetto, the section of the city where the Nazis had confined 500,000 Jews, segregating them from the rest of the Polish people. More than 300,000 Jews had already been sent from the ghetto to be killed in the death camp of Treblinka. The remaining Jews were being rounded up.

In the cellar, Katznelson sat between two men, Guzshik and Gitterman. They pressed close together, silent. Katznelson lit a candle. The other two men looked away from him; their pain was too great to share. But there was also an old man, more than 80 years old, in the cellar that day, an old man who looked straight at Katznelson, though Katznelson had never before seen him. When Katznelson blew out the candle, Guzshik called Katznelson's name. The old man whispered: "The name that I have just heard is familiar to me. About fifty years ago, I had a colleague here in Warsaw, by the name of Binyamin Katznelson. He was a great scholar and fine Jew. . . . They say that he had a son here in Warsaw."

"This is his son," the other men told him.

The old man began to recite a poem. Katznelson recognized it. His father had written the poem 50 years earlier. Katznelson was stunned. He felt as if a ghost were speaking to him. The next day, the old man was murdered in his home by the SS, the Nazi security police.

But Katznelson survived the Warsaw ghetto to bear witness for the old man and for other Jews whom he loved. His wife and two of his sons had been cruelly exterminated. His students had been killed, his entire community destroyed. He, too, would later die in a death camp. But while he could, he continued to write, making it his mission to proclaim the depths of Jewish suffering to the world.

Yitzhak Katznelson was born in July 1886 in the town of Karelitz in the Minsk district of Belorussia. Both his mother and father were the descendants of rabbis and scholars. When Katznelson was eight, his family moved to Poland and two years later settled in Łódź. His father, a rabbi and Hebrew teacher, had a tremendous love and knowledge of both Jewish and secular learning. The young Katznelson was educated in his father's school but had to stop studying before he was 13 because of the family's financial difficulties. He found work as a clerk and as an apprentice in a textile factory. Later he became a teacher of Hebrew and founded his own innovative school, which included religious and Hebrew studies as well as physical education and music.

Katznelson wrote his first play, *Dreyfus and Esterhazy*, at the age of 12. Later he wrote Hebrew literature for children as well as poems and plays. He pioneered the Hebrew theater and was held in esteem by other Hebrew writers of his time.

Happily married to a woman named Channah, he had three sons whom he adored. He was a man with a cheerful disposition who wrote poems of joy. His happiness, however, was short lived. On September 1, 1939, World War II began. On September 8, the Germans invaded Łódź. All Jewish institutions were shut down. Jewish leaders were arrested and tortured, Katznelson's school was taken over by the Gestapo, the Nazi secret police, and it was later used as Gestapo headquarters.

As a community leader, Katznelson was in extreme danger. On September 8, he went into hiding in Łódź. Katznelson's wife persuaded him to escape to Warsaw, which had the largest population of Jews in Poland and would be a safer place for him to hide. On December 4, 1939, the Nazis expelled Katznelson's wife and children from Łódź. They joined Katznelson in Warsaw. There the family was forced to survive under excruciating conditions in the ghetto. There was little food or water and much cold and overcrowding; tens of thousands of people in the ghetto died from disease and starvation.

Fifty-four-year-old Katznelson began to work in the ghetto with a group of young Zionist-socialist pioneers called Dror, the Hebrew word for freedom. These young people refused to submit to Nazi humiliation. Instead, they engaged in cultural and resistance activities. Katznelson published poems in their newsletter, began a drama society, taught Hebrew and Bible studies in an underground high school in the ghetto, and wrote articles for Dror's underground newspaper. He used his creative powers to join the group in fighting the despair of living in a desperate situation where Jews were tortured and murdered every day.

Katznelson wrote his poems and articles in Yiddish, the language of the common Jew in eastern Europe. As soon as he finished a poem, he quickly read it to others. Katznelson felt that his purpose was to be the voice of his generation, a poet of the people.

While in the ghetto, Katznelson managed to publish a play. On June 22, 1941, *Job,* copied by Dror on a duplicating machine, appeared in print—the only book published by Jews in Nazi-occupied Poland.

Nazi security police (SS) walk by a burning building during the Warsaw ghetto uprising in 1943. (Yad VaShem)

Meanwhile, conditions in Warsaw continued to worsen. On July 22, 1942, most of the ghetto's occupants were deported to Treblinka, a death camp in Poland, not far from Warsaw. They had been told that they were being resettled in the eastern territories and that anybody who boarded the train voluntarily would receive 4 kilos (about 10 pounds) of bread and 1 kilogram of jam. Many starving Jews had assembled for the transport.

Friends provided Katznelson with a document that gave him protection from the deportation as a needed factory worker. But this privileged status did not protect his wife and two younger sons, Ben Zion and Binyamin, who were deported on August 14, 1942, and killed in the Treblinka death camp. Although he and his son Zvi successfully escaped subsequent deportations, he was a broken man.

Then, in spring 1943, the remaining Jews in the ghetto rebelled. On the eve of Passover, the SS ordered the destruction of the ghetto. The remaining Jewish inhabitants desperately fought back. More than 1,000 Jewish fighters battled German troops, blowing up their tanks and forcing the Germans to retreat. But the Nazis returned with more troops, tanks, and ammunition. The uprising was quashed after almost four full weeks of resistance. By May 16, 1943, after fierce house-to-house fighting, the Germans deported the remaining Jews to killing centers or concentration camps.

On May 22, 1943, Katznelson and his son were given forged Honduran passports by friends. Because of these documents, instead of being sent to Treblinka, in May 1943, Katznelson and his son were sent to Vittel, an internment camp in eastern France. One month later, in June 1943, the Nazis destroyed the Warsaw ghetto, burning it to the ground.

In Vittel, Katznelson wrote an epic poem, *The Song of the Murdered Jewish People,* and the *Vittel Diary,* which recounts his three-and-one-half years in the Warsaw ghetto. Both the diary and the poem are unique in their raw emotion—the writer's display of overwhelming love for his people and of hatred for their enemies is clear.

In his diary, written between May 22 and September 16, 1943, Katznelson begins by describing his life in Vittel camp, which, although more comfortable than the ghetto, gave him no respite from his apprehension and anxiety. He then recounts the hell of his experiences in the Warsaw ghetto. He cries out, laments, and wails: "Men, women, and children, my own with them, all on the selfsame day, were led to their execution. Every time I try to count up these lives, a feeling of madness comes over me . . . and I have to drop it. But the time for me to go insane is not yet."

Katznelson was a man who loved his people like a father. To him, every man and woman who perished was a part of his family. But he also recognizes and accuses the Jewish police who collaborated with the Nazis, beating and arresting fellow Jews. "They are the reproach of all nations, including ours in whose image they were created. . . . I myself, cannot really believe they seized hold of these infants by their legs and smashed their skulls on the stones, against trees, or against the hard sods of earth. Yet that is what they did. There are no more Jewish children in Europe."

He recounts countless scenes of excruciating brutality: a barber who cuts the hair of a Nazi who will later shoot him dead; a mother who pleads for her violinist son's life only to have him killed alongside her.

He mourns his family: ". . . my tender Binyamin, a young child, caused me to be born anew, just as I had once caused him to be born; and I rejoiced, rejoiced exceedingly to be born through him. My sons! How did these villainous Germans tear you away from your noble mother and kill you? Were you murdered separately? You on the one hand, and she, with all that was noble in her, on the other? . . . Oh my noble Channah, my muse."

He also records the Jews' courage. He writes of the Jewish messengers of the Zionist youth group HaShomer Hatzair who reached Warsaw from Vilna, Lithuania, in early 1942 to report the murder of Jews there (see the chapter on Abba Kovner). He tells of the Jewish fighters who resisted and fought back in the Warsaw ghetto, including his son Zvi who attacked a German guard

"My nation was like a wife and like my sons to me. . . . They meant to me all that my spouse and my sons meant. We were one closely knit family. Our lives were bound together body and soul. We were one. Now you have been done to death, all of you! Oh my people!"

—Yitzhak Katznelson

Children in the Warsaw ghetto (Yad VaShem)

at a factory: ". . . we rose up against those German cowards. On the very first day we killed twelve of these evil beasts."

Most of all he judges the German people:

> It was the whole German nation which not only agreed to and desired the murder of the Jewish people, but made all the necessary preparations and created all the facilities.
>
> [Nineteen] million Germans chose this foul beast Hitler. . . . Ninety-nine percent of this evil people chose this insane murderer to be their chancellor.

Yet even in the midst of his despair and anguish, he has a vision of the Jews in America and Palestine surviving and finding a home: "In the not too distant future a great generation will arise, which will outnumber this one, which met so cruel an end at the hands of the foul scum of the human species. Yet, a nation will be born. It will be a Jewish nation, great and numerous."

Katznelson feels compelled to bear witness to the world the suffering of his people:

> There is not a single Jew here who believes that he will be allowed to remain alive. There is not a single Jew who will remain alive to serve as a living memorial over the graves of the millions that have been murdered. . . . The whole world must know what happened. A whole nation has been murdered in broad daylight before its very eyes, and no one has ventured to utter a word.

Such is the testimony of the *Vittel Diary*.

Katznelson penned his great poem *The Song of the Murdered Jewish People* between October 3, 1943, and January 18, 1944, while he was in Vittel. The poem, dedicated to the memory of his wife and his brother Berl, who also perished in the camps, is a threnody, a dirge or song of lamentation.

The poem is an outpouring of grief for the tragedy that has overtaken his people. As in the *Vittel Diary,* he is a father crying for his wife, his children, and his people.

The poem is composed of 15 sections, or cantos, each with 15 stanzas of 4 long lines. With force and simplicity, the poem portrays the agony of the Jews: suffering children in orphanages, deportations, the Jewish uprising in the ghetto, and the total destruction of the Jews in the ghetto.

In the beginning of the poem, the poet is exhorted to sing to God in spite of all that has occurred:

> Sing! Take your light, hollow harp in hand,
> Strike hard with heavy fingers, like pain-filled hearts
> On its thin chords. Sing the last song.
> Sing of the last Jews on Europe's soil.

But with all of the tragedy that has befallen him and his people, the poet does not feel he can sing:

> How can I sing? How can I lift my head?
> My wife, my Benzionke and Yomele—a baby—
>   deported . . .
> They are not with me, yet they never leave me.
> O dark shadows of my brightest lights, O cold, blind
>   shadows!

Still, the poet complies.

> I play. I sat down low on the ground,
> I played and sang sadly: O my people!
> Millions of Jews stood around me and heard,
> Millions of murdered—a great throng—stood listening.

In the midst of his despair, he forces himself to sing. The dead are his audience and his reason for singing, his reason for crying out. He has a sacred task: to acknowledge the dead, to honor their memory, to be their voice.

Like a biblical prophet who feels unequal to the task God has set before him, so too the poet is reluctant to perform the duty he feels is required of him, yet he must—he must sing of his murdered people, his family.

The poet, steeped in Jewish learning, compares himself to these prophets: "And Ezekiel himself . . . would have wrung his hands like me . . . Like me he would cast back his head helplessly." He cries out to them, but no prophet or biblical hero was ever called upon to endure such torments. The biblical Isaiah did not have to endure what a young orphan boy in Warsaw did: ". . . Isaiah, you were not as small, not as great, / Not as good, not as true, not as faithful as he." As the literary critic James Young says, the newly murdered Jews displace the biblical prophets as new archetypes or models of suffering.

The torture and humiliation of the Jews was unprecedented. One section of the poem relates the story of a pious rabbi forced to open his mouth to allow a German soldier to spit into it: "'Look, look and learn, you dirty Jews, see how one spits—' / And the German spat into the rabbi's mouth: 'Swallow it!' / The rabbi did. . . ."

The poet is reeling in shock from what he has witnessed. He cries out: "O heavens, I praised you, exalted you, in all my songs. . . . O blue heavens, why are you so blue and beautiful while we are being murdered?"

The poet continually identifies with his people. And he knows that he will not escape their cruel fate:

> We all knew it, the fish in the water, the birds on the roof,
> The gentiles around us: We are being killed, all of us killed!
> For no reason! Nothing can be done! The die is cast:
> To destroy the Jewish people, cut it down root and branch . . .

At the close of the poem, all the Jews of Europe are destroyed: "Never will a Jewish mother cradle a baby. Jews will not die or be born . . . Woe is unto me, nobody is left . . . There was a people and it is no more. There was a people and it is . . . Gone . . ."

Katznelson is the devastated witness of the tragic destruction of the Jewish people in Europe. And their destruction is his own.

After *The Song of the Murdered Jewish People* was completed, Katznelson and a friend, Miriam Novitch, also imprisoned in Vittel, hid the poem in three small bottles and buried them deep in the ground under the roots of a pine tree. The *Vittel Diary* was sewn into the dress of a laundress and smuggled out of the camp.

On April 19, 1944, two months after completing the poem, Katznelson and his son were sent from Vittel to a transit camp at Drancy. On April 29, 1944, he and his son were sent to Auschwitz where they were killed on May 3, 1944.

On September 12, Vittel was liberated by British and U.S. soldiers. After the war, Novitch herself unearthed *The Song of the Murdered Jewish People*. The *Vittel Diary* was also recovered. But the poet and his son were dead, burned in the furnaces of Auschwitz.

Chronology

July 1886	Yitzhak Katznelson born in Karelitz in the Minsk district of Belorussia
1896	settles in Łódź, Poland
September 8, 1939	Łódź overrun by Germans
November	Katznelson escapes to Warsaw
June 22, 1941	publishes the play *Job* in the Warsaw ghetto
July 22	mass deportation of Jews in the Warsaw ghetto begins
August 14	Katznelson's wife and two children deported to Treblinka
May 22, 1943	Katznelson taken to Vittel with his son Zvi
May 22–September 16	writes *Vittel Diary*
October 1943–January 1944	writes *The Song of the Murdered Jewish People*
April 29, 1944	Katznelson and his son taken to Auschwitz
May 3	Yitzhak Katznelson and his son killed at Auschwitz
September 12	Vittel liberated
end of 1944	manuscripts of *The Song of the Murdered Jewish People* and *Vittel Diary* are recovered

Further Reading

Yitzhak Katznelson's Works

The Song of the Murdered Jewish People. Translated by Noah Rosenbloom. Israel: Ghetto Fighters' House, Kibbutz Hameuchad Publishing House, 1980. A book-length poem lamenting the suffering of the Jewish people. The introduction provides an insightful analysis of the poem.
Vittel Diary. Translated by Myer Cohen. Israel: Ghetto Fighters' House, Kibbutz Hameuchad Publishing House, 1972. A diary of Katznelson's experience in the Warsaw ghetto.

Works About Yitzhak Katznelson

Aaron, Frieda. *Bearing the Unbearable: Yiddish and Polish Poetry in the Ghettos and Concentration Camps.* Albany: State University of New York Press, 1990. The role of poetry as testimony and as a means of moral defiance. Includes numerous references to Katznelson's writings.
Wigoder, Geoffrey. *Dictionary of Jewish Biography.* New York: Simon and Schuster, 1991. Includes a brief but detailed biographical sketch of Katznelson.

Abba Kovner, a poet, survived the war as a guerrilla fighter. (Yad VaShem)

Abba Kovner

(1918–1987)

Few people believed 11-year-old Tema Katz. In November 1941, she claimed that she was one of the thousands of Jews of Vilna taken to Ponary, 20 miles away. There the Nazis forced the Jews into a ditch surrounded by barbed wire and shot them dead in the frigid earth. Lime was poured over their bodies before the next thousand bodies were dragged into the trenches and shot. But the rifles had missed Tema. She was still alive. She managed to crawl her way out of the upper layer of the cold pit and stumble through 20 miles of frozen forest back to the Vilna ghetto.

A woman named Yehudit Streuch said that she too had witnesssed the horrifying scene in Ponary: The Jews were being murdered in cold blood.

Most people did not believe Tema and Yehudit's words. Surely these were rumors, fabricated stories. Surely the Germans were taking the Jews away for labor, as the German authorities claimed.

But Abba Kovner believed the girl and woman. Not long after listening to them, he and other members of his youth organization, HaShomer Hatzair, decided that they must take action. It was Kovner who wrote the Vilna proclamation, a call for revolt. It was Kovner and other members of his youth group who saw the impending doom and knew that what had happened at Ponary was not an isolated incident. The Nazis were singling out the Jews, not just of Vilna, but of all of Europe, for mass annihilation. The response that Kovner envisioned to that evil was resistance. Although he knew that Jewish resistance would probably be ineffective, at least the Jews could die with dignity.

Abba Kovner was born in 1918 in Sebastopol, a seaport in the Crimea, on the Black Sea in Russia. Before World War I, his family had been on their way to Palestine (now Israel) from Lithuania, but because of the outbreak of the war, they had been unable to reach their destination. Later his family returned to Vilna, the capital of Lithuania, which after World War I was within Poland's borders. Kovner attended Hebrew high school and joined a socialist youth group, HaShomer Hatzair. He was interested in immigrating to Palestine, but World War II prevented him.

Before 1939, Vilna was a center of Jewish learning, culture, and creativity. Famous Jewish academies thrived. There were groups of Jewish political activists and youth groups, a Jewish newspaper, and Jewish literature. But in July 1940, Lithuania was occupied by the Soviet Union. The Soviets forbade the Jews to meet in any groups, especially in organizations. Then in 1941, the Germans occupied Lithuania as well as much of the Soviet Union. The Lithuanians collaborated with the Nazis in organizing huge anti-Semitic killings. (Anti-Semitism is hatred against and discrimination of Jews.) The Jews of Lithuania were the first community to be exterminated by Nazi mass murders. By November 1941, 47,000 Jews had been taken from Vilna and shot at Ponary. On September 1, 1943, the last thousands of Jews remaining in Vilna were taken to the death camps. By the end of the war, more than 200,000 Lithuanian Jews had been killed.

At first, when the Germans occupied Vilna in 1941, Kovner and some other youth-group members were hidden by the mother superior in the convent of the Dominican Sisters, about 3 miles outside Vilna. Then, suspecting that the Nazis intended to murder the entire Jewish population of Europe, Kovner and others decided to fight back. On January 1, 1942, at a meeting of 150 youth-group members, Kovner read the proclamation he had written, titled "Let Us Not Go Like Sheep to Slaughter." In that work, as well as in much of the poetry and prose he would later write, he shows a commitment to his people, and a willingness to fight for them.

In the manifesto he pleads with his comrades and the remaining people in the ghetto to see the truth of the horror that was befalling them:

> Of the 80,000 Jews in the "Jerusalem of Lithuania" (Vilna) only 20,000 have remained. Before our eyes they tore from us our parents, our brothers, and sisters.

Kovner is in the top row, middle. His wife Vitka stands on the far right. (Yad VaShem)

Where are the hundreds of men who were taken away for work by the Lithuanian snatchers? Where are the naked women and children who were taken from us in the night of terror of the provokatzia [provocation]? . . . All the roads of the Gestapo lead to Ponary. And Ponary is death. Doubters! Cast off all illusions. Your children, your husbands and your wives are no longer alive. Ponary is not a camp—all are shot there.

According to historian Dina Porat, Kovner's document was a turning point in the Jews' comprehension of the catastrophe that was occurring. Kovner and his group sent out messengers to warn other Jewish communities, including those of Warsaw and Białystok, of Hitler's plans. But most Jews could not believe that the Nazis were intending mass murder.

In 1943, Kovner became the leader of a combat group, the United Partisan Organization, that fought in the Vilna forest. The group took part in sabotage operations against the Nazis, including blowing up three German trains. Kovner and his future wife, Vitka, were responsible for at least one of these explosions. In one incident, Kovner acquired dynamite, and Vitka hid it on the train tracks outside the ghetto. The train was destroyed. In retaliation, the Germans punished a nearby Polish village, never imagining that it was the Jews who were responsible for the act of resistance.

In 1945, after the war, Kovner went to Italy where he helped organize a movement called Bricha, which means "flee" in Hebrew. Palestine, under British rule, had restricted Jewish immigration. Kovner's group's mission was to help thousands of

> "Brothers! It is better to fall as free fighters than to live by the grace of the murderers. Resist! To the last breath."
>
> —Abba Kovner

Jewish refugees flee to Palestine. On July 17, 1945, at a meeting in Italy of Jewish resistance fighters, members of the Jewish Brigade, and other combatants of eastern Europe, Kovner called on the fighters to "transform the Jewish tragedy from a sea of tears and blood into a force of revolutionary strength, to ensure that our liberation movement will encompass the entire life of the survivors, and inspire them with one single great and urgent task—rescue."

Later in 1945, Kovner went to Palestine. He planned to return to Europe to arrange the rescue of more Jews and also to take part in revenge operations against former Nazis, plans that included poisoning the water in major German cities. However, on his way to Europe, Kovner was arrested by the British secret police and imprisoned in Egypt. While there, he wrote the poem "Until There Is No More Light," a 150-page epic describing a night in the life of the Jewish partisans in the Vilna forest. Later he was moved to a Jerusalem prison from which the Haganah, the Jewish underground army of Palestine, freed him.

In Israel, he and Vitka, by now his wife, became members of Kibbutz Ein HaHoresh. (A kibbutz is a collective agricultural settlement in which members pool their resources.) During Israel's War of Independence in 1948, Kovner was cultural officer of an elite military unit, in charge of daily communications.

Since then, Kovner has written more than 14 books of poetry and prose in Hebrew. Some have been translated into English, including *My Little Sister, A Parting from the South,* and *A Canopy in the Desert.* All three are book-length poems that combine personal and historical material.

My Little Sister is the book that most directly concerns itself with the Holocaust; however, as his translator Shirley Kaufman has noted, all of Kovner's work concerns itself with the trauma of the Holocaust. Published in 1967, *My Little Sister* is a major poem sequence consisting of 46 passages in 5 sections. It opens with a young girl seeking shelter in a convent during the

In Ponary, Jews, heads covered, being led to be murdered (Yad VaShem)

Holocaust. Her life and death represent the lives and deaths of thousands of people like her during the war.

Kovner was inspired to write the poem after walking down a street in Tel Aviv and hearing a woman repeatedly scream. Later he realized that the cry had come from a maternity hospital and that the woman had been in labor. He also realized that nobody else in the street seemed to notice her screams or her pain. And suddenly in his mind, he was back in Europe during the war, when the world seemed to ignore the suffering of the Jews.

My Little Sister records the pain of the Jewish people during the Holocaust. Kovner mourns not just one girl but all the "little sisters" who were persecuted during the war. Personally, he mourns his mother who died at Ponary. (Kovner himself had no sisters.) Vitka, his wife, says that the poem expresses Kovner's guilt and suffering at being unable to save his mother from death at the hands of the Nazis. The poem is also a testament to Tema Katz, the girl who returned half-crazed from Ponary. As Shirley

Kaufman writes in her introduction to *My Little Sister and Selected Poems,* the vision of Tema Katz "haunts every line he writes. She appears in poem after poem as daughter, sister, my love, you, never by name."

Kovner has observed: "Poetry is, in a sense, a request for pardon for what we do in our lives, and for what was done to us. If there is any moral meaning to poetry in general, perhaps, this is it. A way of asking forgiveness for the evil in human existence."

My Little Sister is an attempt to reckon with the evil that befell the Jewish people as well as an elegy for those who died. The central image of the poem is the little sister, an allusion to the biblical Song of Songs. In the Song of Songs, God is the bridegroom and the little sister symbolizes the Jewish people. Kovner's poem employs this archetype.

According to Kaufman, many of the passages in the poem are written in the style of the *piyut,* traditional religious hymns. Kovner's father, a poor landlord, used to sing these hymns, especially on the Sabbath. The rhythm and sounds of those ancient melodies returned to Kovner when he wrote.

The poem, divided into five sections, begins with a young girl's desperate attempt to hide in a convent. The little sister bangs on the gates of the convent, but the iron chime is "caught in a mass of ice" and will not ring. The world is indifferent to the girl's suffering. Finally the bell rings and is answered by nine nuns. The nuns look at the little sister, seeing "ashes that speak." Unlike the mother superior of the convent, these nuns lack real compassion for the girl. They do not offer the girl a safe harbor, only a temporary port—"Only a folded sail in a storm," as Kovner writes.

In Part 2 of the epic, the poet asks: "How mourn a city / whose people are dead and whose dead are alive / in the heart." The poet himself keeps the dead alive by remembering them, by linking himself with the victims.

In Part 3, a tragic wedding is celebrated. In passage 28 the little sister sits happy at her bridegroom's table. Father twists the braids of the challah, the Jewish bread used for ritual events. "Our father took his bread, bless God, / forty years from one oven. He never imagined / a whole people could rise in the ovens / and the world, with God's help, go on." The people are the Jews, killed in the ovens of the camps.

Then Kovner envisions the sister sitting alone. The voice of the bridegroom speaks from "the hideout of mourners": "We will set the table without you; / the marriage contract will be written in stone." The little sister is a bride missing from her own wedding, a victim of the killings. The Jews are left forlorn, at a total loss. "With what— / with what, little sister, / shall we weave and draw the dream / now?"

In Part 4, passage 41, one of the most difficult in the book, the poet attempts to talk to the dead. He tries to invent a language for the dead, some way of reaching them, of bringing them back to life. In a letter to translator Kaufman, Kovner explains the poem: "She stands on the other side and does not hear me, does not understand my language. My God! There must be a language which will make a bridge between us. A language of the living which the dead will also hear and understand."

In Part 5, the war is over, and everything has been lost. In passage 44, the poet merges with his sister. "Tomorrow they will be the first to forget: / they will cover up my blood." The poet's voice moves from the third person "she" to the first person "we" as the poet becomes one with his sister and one with the forgotten victims.

Suddenly, in passage 45, we are introduced to a second sister, a sister who died at the age of two hours.

> "For me poetry is not merely an ecstatic experience, but an enduring attempt to turn ashes into an eternal light."
>
> —Abba Kovner

"My sister did not scream. / She was not introduced to the world." The mother mourns another sister who never came into the world. The poet mourns for all the little sisters whose lives were cut short during the Holocaust.

And the poem ends: "no one will carry my mother's bier with me / no one will come close to my mother's bier with me."

The poet is alone with the weight of his suffering. He states that he cannot carry his mother's coffin, for she had none. Instead he bears the stand her coffin would have been placed on before her burial. In a sense, he is the stand for his mother's coffin. He alone marks his mother's death.

Kovner tries to speak for the dead, to rescue what cannot be rescued, to understand what cannot be understood. Thus, there is often ambiguity in his poems. As Kaufman writes in her introduction to *A Canopy in the Desert*, "There are times when not to understand, or not to understand completely, is more important, more instant, more significant, than total comprehension."

Kovner once said, "When I write, I am like a man praying." He wrote for his community, to awaken those who are alive and give voice to those who are dead.

In 1970, Kovner received the Israel Prize, Israel's most prestigious award. He died of cancer in 1987 and is buried at Kibbutz Ein HaHoresh where his wife, Vitka, still lives. On her wall is a large photograph of Kovner—fighter, husband, father, and writer.

Chronology

1918	Abba Kovner born in the Crimea
January 1, 1942	reads his proclamation, "Do Not Go Like Sheep to the Slaughter"
1943	becomes leader of United Partisan Organization, a resistance combat group
1944	organizes missions to rescue Jews and send them to Palestine
1945	arrives in Palestine; arrested on his way to Europe to continue his rescue work; jailed in an Egyptian prison
1949	publishes *A Parting from the South* in Hebrew
1967	publishes *My Little Sister*
1970	publishes *A Canopy in the Desert* in Hebrew; receives Israel Prize, a literary award
1987	Abba Kovner dies; buried at Kibbutz Ein HaHoresh

Further Reading

Abba Kovner's Works

"Address to the Jewish Brigade," in *The Catastrophe of European Jewry*. Edited by Yisrael Gutman and Livia Rotkirchen. Jerusalem: Yad Vashem, 1976. Kovner's speech called for illegal Jewish immigration to Palestine.

A Canopy in the Desert. Translated by Shirley Kaufman. Pittsburgh: University of Pittsburgh Press, 1973. Selected poems including "A Parting from the South," "A Canopy in the Desert," and "My Little Sister."

"Do Not Go Like Sheep to Slaughter," in *Documents on the Holocaust*. Edited by Yitzak Arad, Yisrael Gutman, and Abraham Margaliot. Jerusalem: Yad Vashem, 1981. Kovner's manifesto was the first call for a Jewish armed uprising.

My Little Sister and Selected Poems. Translated by Shirley Kaufman. Oberlin, Ohio: Oberlin College Press, 1986. Kaufman, an American poet who lives in Israel, has translated Kovner's work with love. Her introduction gives the reader a feeling for Kovner the man as well as insight into his work.

Works About Abba Kovner

Alexander, Edward. "Abba Kovner: Poet of Holocaust and Rebirth." *Midstream* (October 1977), pp. 50–59. A thoughtful analysis of Kovner's work, especially *My Little Sister*.

Ginor, Zvia Ben Yosef. "The Sheliah Tsibur As a Poetic Persona: Abba Kovner's Self-Portrait." *Prooftexts* 15 (1995), pp. 227–47. Academic criticism (from Johns Hopkins University Press) of Kovner's work.

Porat, Dina. "The Vilna Proclamation of January 1, 1942, in Historical Perspective." *Yad VaShem Studies* 25 (1996), pp. 99–136. Detailed explanation of the events that led Kovner to write his famous proclamation.

Primo Levi as a young man. An Italian chemist, he wrote about his survival in Auschwitz. (Yad VaShem)

Primo Levi

(1919–1987)

On the night of January 18, 1945, Hitler's Nazi soldiers were evacuating Auschwitz, the concentration camp in Poland where more than a million Jews had already been killed. Twenty-four-year-old Primo Levi had been imprisoned there for almost a year. The Russians, the Allied army liberating eastern Europe from Nazi oppression, were said to be close, perhaps 60 miles away. The next day, the Nazi soldiers marched off with almost all of the prisoners in Auschwitz. The Jewish prisoners were hopeful that they would, at last, find freedom.

Levi was left behind. Sick with scarlet fever, he was too weak to leave the camp. From his infirmary bed, Levi could hear the hum of the prisoners' excitement at leaving the concentration camp. That cold January 18, 1945, he and the other sick prisoners were left behind without food, water, lights, electricity, or heat. The temperature outside reached −5°.

For 10 days, Levi and his companions stayed in the camp. Many died from sickness, exhaustion, and cold. Their bodies lay on the snow or on the floor of the infirmary. But with the help of a cast-iron stove for heat and the food he and some fellow prisoners were able to scavenge, Levi survived.

> Levi's best friend, Alberto, died on the forced march from Auschwitz. So did almost every other prisoner, about 20,000 in all, from cold or exhaustion or from being shot by Nazis for stepping out of line.
> Levi survived by being left behind.
> Although he was a chemist, not a writer, by trade the careful observation and analysis he had learned as a chemistry student allowed him to meticulously describe the horrifying experience of being in Auschwitz. The need to testify about Auschwitz transformed Levi into a writer.

Primo Levi was born on July 31, 1919, in Turin, an industrial city in northern Italy. Both his parents had degrees in engineering. Levi, too, had a strong interest in science. In 1937, he enrolled in the University of Turin to major in chemistry. Soon after, he found himself affected by anti-Jewish policies.

Levi had grown up in a middle-class assimilated household. Jews in Italy at that time composed only one-tenth of 1 percent of the entire population, a tiny fraction. In fact, while growing up, Levi had not felt particularly Jewish.

Suddenly, on September 12, 1938, the Jews of Italy were targeted for persecution. Under the influence of their Nazi allies, the Italian government passed racist laws. Jews were forbidden to study in universities or to teach in state and private schools. Further laws prohibited Jews from marrying non-Jews, from serving in the military, and from working as journalists or in public service. Levi was allowed to complete his studies but his degree marked him "of the Jewish race."

In late 1943, the Italian government fell. The Nazis conquered northern Italy and installed the former leader of Italy, Benito Mussolini, to rule in collaboration with them. Southern Italy was occupied by Allied forces. The country was divided by war.

In the north, Levi and his friends joined the Italian resistance, working to fight the Nazis. But before their first mission, on December 13, 1943, Levi and two fellow partisans were captured by Italian soldiers who supported the Nazis. In late January 1944, Levi was sent to Fossoli, a detention camp in northern Italy. On February 22, Levi boarded the train that would take him to Auschwitz, a concentration camp in southern Poland. On that train were 500 Jewish prisoners from Italy. On their arrival at Auschwitz, all but 29 women and 95 men were killed in the gas chambers. As Levi tells us in his first book, *Survival in Auschwitz*, "The night swallowed them up, purely and simply."

Levi and a small number of other prisoners were kept alive in order to work for the Nazi war effort. Like almost all Jewish prisoners, Levi's arm was tattooed. Prisoners were identified by number, not name. He was number 174,517.

A transport arriving at Auschwitz (Yad VaShem)

Auschwitz transport arrival, May 27, 1944 (Yad VaShem)

In Auschwitz, Levi suffered from severe malnutrition and exhaustion. He witnessed cruelty, beatings, hangings, and selections for the gas chambers.

But Levi's occupation of chemist allowed him to survive. About 4 miles away from the gas chambers and crematoriums of Auschwitz where thousands of Nazi victims were gassed and burned daily was the Buna Rubber plant. This German factory manufactured rubber for the Nazi war effort. There were so few qualified chemists that prisoners were needed to work there. Levi passed an examination in organic chemistry, which allowed him to work in a laboratory in the Buna plant and survive the war.

After the war, Levi returned to his hometown, to the house where he had been born. His mother had survived the war in hiding. Levi returned to work as a chemist. But he was impelled to write, to testify about what he had seen, to speak for those who had been killed, to be a witness for those who had no chance to defend themselves.

Levi married Lucia Morpurgo in 1947 and later had two children. In the 1950s he was busy raising his family and working as an industrial chemist. During this time, he was also writing. In 1958, Levi's *If This Is a Man* (later titled *Survival in Auschwitz*) was published in Italy.

The book is a memoir of Levi's time in Auschwitz. He records with precision and with meticulous detail the dehumanizing rules and regulations, the humiliations and pain of being a prisoner.

In such a hostile environment, Levi tells us that "survival without giving up any thing of one's own moral world was granted only to very few superior individuals, made of the stuff of martyrs and saints." But there were those who helped Levi, who showed him that "there still existed a just world outside our own." These people who managed to keep their humanity and self-respect in the face of enormous obstacles are the people whom Levi immortalizes in his book.

There was Lorenzo, an Italian civilian worker, who brought Levi a piece of bread every day for six months. "Thanks to Lorenzo I managed not to forget I myself was a man."

There was Levi's best friend, Alberto, who shared his meager rations with Levi and kept his spirits up. A fellow prisoner, Jean, shared Levi's pleasure when Levi recited the great Italian poem "Ulysses" by Dante while the two were working. The power of the poem allowed Levi temporary respite from his suffering: "For a moment I forget who I am and where I am."

"Nothing belongs to us anymore; they have taken away our clothes, our shoes, even our hair; if we speak, they will not listen to us, and if they listen, they will not understand. They have even taken away our name. . . ."

—Primo Levi

Throughout *Survival in Auschwitz,* Levi's aim is to describe what he saw, not to stand in judgment. His language is sober and measured, reflecting traits he learned as a scientist. Yet the book is incredibly moving. Levi's undramatized account powerfully describes the horror of the camps. It also shows how human relationships sustained Levi there. Although the Nazis had done everything possible to take away the prisoners' humanity, some prisoners refused to lose their dignity.

In Levi's next book, *The Truce,* (also known as *The Reawakening*), he realizes that although he is gone from Auschwitz, he will never be free of his need to speak of it nor free from its horror. The book describes Levi's nine-month journey home after the war in a sequence of adventures. The book begins with four Russian soldiers' arrival at Auschwitz on January 27, 1945.

"Even less do I accept hatred as directed collectively at an ethnic group, for example, all the Germans; if I accepted it, I would feel that I was following the precepts of Nazism, which was founded precisely on national and racial hatred."

—Primo Levi

Levi describes the soldiers' looks of shame and embarrassment at seeing the prisoners looking like walking skeletons, so debased and degraded. After Levi was rescued, the weariness and illness he had been combatting in his quest for survival attacked him with such ferocity that he was unable to stand on his feet. But by that point, the Russians were able to nurse Levi back to health.

In the book, Levi recounts the stories of people after their liberation. One of the most tragic is that of Hurbinek, a three-year-old child who "died in the first days of March 1945, free but not redeemed. Nothing remains of him: he bears witness through these words of mine."

Despite the gravity of what most of these people had lived through, some of the character descriptions are humorous stories of people rediscovering life. For example, Cesare had been deathly ill in the Auschwitz infirmary with Levi, but in the transit camp of Katowice he became a different person—resourceful and lighthearted. Needing money, he successfully sold a shirt by holding his finger over the hole in the collar.

Finally, after much waiting, Levi and the other Italians were taken to Russia, where they waited for months in a small village named Starye Dorogi. Levi recorded some of their adventures there: One night he, Cesare, and some others ventured into the countryside where, despite difficulty in making themselves understood, they managed to trade six plates for a chicken.

But on Levi's return home on October 19, 1945, the traumatic events of Auschwitz return to haunt him. Levi relates that even after he was safe in his bed, a dream returned to him: "I am in the Lager [the German word for "camp"] once more, and nothing is true outside the Lager. All the rest was a brief pause, a deception of the senses. . . ." Although he could appreciate the joy of living, he realized he would never be able to escape the nightmare of Auschwitz.

After the war, Levi returned to work as a chemist. In 1947, he took a job as a chemist at SIVA, a paint factory. In *The Periodic Table,* published in Italian in the spring of 1975, he combined stories of his experiences as a chemist with stories of his past and of Auschwitz. Although the book is called a novel, it is not a traditional one. It is composed of 21 stories, each named after one of the elements of Mendeleev's periodic table, the table of elements used in every chemistry class. Certain elements serve as springboards for Levi's imagination, reminding Levi of an event or character from his past. For example, in the chapter "Argon," Levi describes his ancestors: "The little I know about my ancestors presents many similarities to these gases. . . . Noble, inert, and rare:

their history is quite poor when compared to that of other illustrious Jewish communities in Italy and Europe."

"Vanadium" is a story about Levi's discovery while working as general manager at SIVA in 1967 that a German chemist with whom he was negotiating about a faulty batch of varnish was the same German man who had supervised Levi's slavery in Auschwitz. Levi described writing him a letter tactfully judging the man's behavior: "In the real world the armed exist, they build Auschwitz; and the honest and unarmed clear the road for them. . . ."

The successful reception of *The Periodic Table* marked Levi's arrival as a major Italian writer. After its publication, Levi quit his job and began to devote himself full-time to writing.

In 1982, *If Not Now, When?* appeared. The book, Levi's only novel with a traditional narrative structure, is a tribute to eastern European Jews who tried to resist the Nazis. It tells the story of a group of Jewish resistance fighters who make their way through the Soviet Union, Poland, and Germany hoping to get to Palestine (now Israel).

Moments of Reprieve, published in English in 1986, tells the stories of men who managed to keep their identity in Auschwitz. In his introduction, Levi tells us, "The protagonists of these stories are 'men' beyond all doubt, even if the virtue that allows them to survive and makes them unique is not always one approved of by common morality." For example, Levi recounts teaching a new arrival, Bandi: to survive in the camp Levi told him that one must work as little and as badly as possible. Reluctant at first to lie, by the end of the story, Bandi gives Levi a radish he's stolen: "I've learned. This is for you. It's the first thing I've stolen."

Levi not only wrote fiction and memoirs but also poetry. His early poems, printed privately, were later published with the title, *Shema,* the Hebrew word for "listen," the first word in one of the most important Jewish prayers.

The title poem, also the epigraph of *Survival in Auschwitz,* warns the readers who are "safe in their warm houses" to remember human suffering. In 1984, the *Collected Poems* were published in English.

In his last book, *The Drowned and the Saved,* a collection of eight essays, Levi moved from witness to judge and insisted most forcefully that all of us must judge and must not stand by. He who stands by and allows evil to occur is guilty. "The failure to speak the truth about the death camps is one of the major collective crimes of the German people. Those who could have failed to live up to their moral responsibilities." Levi expresses his worry that the world hasn't learned from the trauma of the Holocaust and that such an event may happen again because the world has not paid sufficient attention.

Primo Levi died on April 11, 1987, in the house where he was born. He fell to his death from the stairwell of his third-floor apartment. Levi was thought to have suffered from depression. He was also fatigued from the strain of caring for both his own invalid mother and his ill mother-in-law. Many speculate that Levi killed himself. "Primo Levi died at Auschwitz forty years later," author Elie Wiesel said.

We do not know exactly how Levi died. We do know that Levi was an extraordinary man, a prize-winning author, and a man who refused to hate because he believed that to hate was to engage in conduct unacceptable to reason.

Instead Levi strove to communicate, to testify, to tell his story to the largest number of people. Of Primo Levi, it can be truly said, "he was a man."

Chronology

July 31, 1919	Primo Levi born in Turin, Italy
1938	first racial laws against Jews are passed
July 1943	Levi joins partisan forces
December 13	captured by the Fascist militia
January 1944	sent to Fossoli
February 22	deported to Auschwitz
January 27, 1945	liberated from Auschwitz
October 19	returns to Turin
1947	begins work as chemist at SIVA, a small paint company
1958	*If This Is a Man* published in Italy
1963	Levi publishes *The Reawakening*
1975	publishes *The Periodic Table*
1977	retires from SIVA; begins writing full-time
1984	English translation of *The Periodic Table* published
1987	Primo Levi falls to his death
1988	*The Drowned and the Saved* published in English

Further Reading

Primo Levi's Works

Collected Poems: New Edition. Translated by Ruth Feldman and Brian Swann. London: Faber and Faber, 1992. These poems convey intellectual, moral, and social messages. Many include Levi's memories of persecution.

The Drowned and the Saved. Translated by Raymond Rosenthal. New York: Random House, 1989. A collection of essays where Levi warns that people must fight against evil.

If Not Now, When? Translated by William Weaver. New York: Viking Penguin, 1995. A novel about Jewish armed resistance.

Moments of Reprieve. New York: Viking Penguin, 1995. These stories show moments when Auschwitz prisoners express their humanity, refusing to be victims.

The Periodic Table. Translated by Raymond Rosenthal. New York: Schocken Books, 1995. The author writes tales about his life, using the elements of the Periodic Table as a motif.

The Reawakening. New York: Simon and Schuster, 1995. Survivors of Auschwitz return to their native Italy after their liberation.

Survival in Auschwitz. New York: Simon and Schuster, 1995. An account of the writer's 10 months in a death camp.

Works About Primo Levi

Cicioni, Maria. *Primo Levi, Bridges of Knowledge.* Oxford: Berg Publishers, 1995. Comprehensive biography and literary analysis.

Patruno, Nicholas. *Understanding Primo Levi.* Columbia: University of South Carolina Press, 1995. A literary analysis of Levi's major work.

Rudolf, Anthony. *At an Uncertain Hour: Primo Levi's War Against Oblivion.* London: The Menard Press, 1990. A short tribute to Levi's work.

Tarrow, Susan, ed. *Reason and Light: Essays on Primo Levi.* Ithaca, N.Y.: Cornell University, 1990. Collected essays by academic experts brought together for a symposium on Levi's work.

Poet Hannah Senesh left Palestine and parachuted into Europe to try to save Hungarian Jews. (Yad VaShem)

Hannah Senesh

(1921–1944)

The engine roared as Hannah Senesh waited her turn. A parachute was stowed on her back, a gun strapped to her side. She jumped from the plane into the moonlit night, plummeting in free fall before her parachute opened and she floated a mile to the ground in Yugoslavia.

Reaching the ground did not guarantee her safety. It was March 13, 1944. The German leader, Adolf Hitler, and his Nazi troops had already invaded Yugoslavia as well as most of western Europe. He had now begun his advance into Hungary, Senesh's native country.

Senesh's mission was to try to rescue the Jews of Hungary before Hitler reached them. One of the Jews she hoped to save was her mother, Catherine. But time was against her.

Parachuting directly into Hungary had become too dangerous. Instead Senesh and her comrades made their way through the Yugoslavian countryside, past enemy fire, through the dark forests on their way to Hungary.

On June 9, 1944, before crossing the Hungarian border, Senesh scrawled a poem on a scrap of paper and handed it to Reuven Dafne, her comrade. Senesh was captured soon after crossing the border. Months later, she was killed. But that poem, "Blessed Is the Match," is still recited by almost every child in Israel.

Hannah Senesh was born in Hungary on July 17, 1921, in Budapest. Her father, a well-known playwright, died when she was six. Her mother Catherine nonetheless managed to provide Senesh and her brother George with an idyllic childhood that included traveling in the countryside, vacationing at beautiful lakes, and attending museum exhibits and concerts.

Senesh started writing as a young girl. At an early age, she won awards in school for her poetry and essays. In 1934, at the age of 13, she began keeping a diary and continued to do so throughout her years in Palestine until she was 23.

Senesh's diary begins with her life as a young girl in Budapest. She described concerts, paintings, books, boys, and on August 3, 1936, her desire to be a writer: "I still long to be a writer. It's my constant wish. I don't know whether it's simply a desire for praise and fame, but I do know it is such a marvelous feeling to write something well that I think it is worth struggling to become a writer."

Senesh's entries are interspersed with comments about the political situation in Europe. She noted the shadow of war but kept hoping that the Nazis would be stopped before they could obliterate the enchanted life she and her family led in Hungary.

In September 1937, however, her personal life collided with history. When Senesh was nominated to be secretary of her high school literary society, the girls in the class ahead of her rejected her as a candidate because she was Jewish. This bigotry caused Senesh great pain.

A surge of anti-Semitism swept across Europe. In Hungary, the first Jewish Bill, passed in 1938, limited the number of Jews who could engage in certain professions. It stated that "the expansion of the Jews is as detrimental to the nation as it is dangerous. We must take steps to defend ourselves against their propagation."

"We're living through indescribably tense days," Senesh wrote in her diary in September 1938 when the Germans were poised to invade Czechoslovakia, a neighboring country. Yet she kept hoping that the Nazis would be stopped. "Though the atmosphere is explosive, I still believe there will be peace."

Finally though, she could not deny the Nazi menace and the hatred towards Jews sweeping through Europe. In October 1938, Senesh declared herself a Zionist, someone who believed that the Jewish people should have their own homeland. Soon after, she dedicated herself to settling in Palestine. In her journal, she noted that she had found a mission for herself, a sense of purpose. She began to keep her diary in Hebrew, in order to improve her command of the language that was spoken among Jews in Palestine.

On September 1, 1939, war broke out in Europe when Germany invaded Poland. With great difficulty, 18-year-old Senesh was still able to arrange her passage to Palestine on board the ship *Bessarabia*. Senesh begged her mother to join her. Her mother, though, continued to believe that anti-Jewish sentiment in Hungary would recede and refused to leave her home. Senesh left for Palestine on September 13, 1939.

Senesh's diary during these years is an invaluable chronicle of life in Palestine during World War II.

Palestine, then governed by the British, was an important destination for Jewish refugees from

"One needs to feel that one's life has meaning, that one is needed in this world. . . . Zionism fulfills all this for me. The thought that now occupies my every waking moment is Palestine. Everything in connection with it interests me, everything else is entirely secondary."

—Hannah Senesh

Europe. But on May 17, 1939, in a document known as the White Paper, the British limited the number of Jewish immigrants to 75,000 people over five years. Senesh described her despair at seeing ships of Jewish refugees being turned away from Palestine by the British.

Senesh's goal in Palestine was to help build the struggling settlement. Between 1939 and 1941, she studied poultry farming at Nahalal Training school. In 1941, she joined Kibbutz Sdot-Yam. (A kibbutz is a collective settlement based on socialist principles of equality: All members work together and share their resources equally.) Senesh hoped that helping the young kibbutz to grow and prosper would be the realization of all she had worked for since leaving Hungary.

But kibbutz life was not what she had hoped it would be. Senesh's play, *The Violin,* written in early 1942, describes the pain a young kibbutz worker feels when she sacrifices her talent to settle the land. The girl is a violinist who has no time to practice and is afraid she is losing her art. For Senesh, too, kibbutz life was full of sacrifices. She worked long days as a laundress. "I'll try to write a bit, though my hands are nearly frozen," she wrote in her diary. At times she felt that she was wasting herself, not using all of her abilities.

At the same time, reports from Europe became more and more dire. Massacres were reported in Poland. Hitler's power was spreading. Hungary was being threatened. Senesh's worries about the conditions in Europe intruded on her kibbutz life. On January 8, 1943, she wrote, "I feel I must be there during these days in order to help organize youth immigration and also to get my mother out."

Senesh knew she had to act. A million Jews lived in Hungary. She could not sit by while there was the possibility, remote as it was, of saving her people from suffering.

On February 22, 1943, she learned that the British were organizing a group of Jewish soldiers to help fight the Nazis. The squad was to parachute into enemy territory.

In 1943, she was accepted into the special paratrooper unit. Out of 240 trainees, Senesh was one of 3 women.

In January 1944, Senesh was sent to Cairo, Egypt, for training, which included armed and unarmed combat, Morse code, assembling and taking apart radio transmitters, and other skills. For the British, the purpose of the mission was to gather information about German troop movements and enemy strength and to help Allied prisoners of war. After accomplishing that aim, they would allow the Jews to rescue their own people—the aim closest to Senesh's heart.

In Cairo, Senesh and the members of her crew—Yonah Rosen, Abba Berdichev, Reuven Dafne, Yoel Palgi, and Peretz Goldstein—were eager to leave for Europe, but their mission was delayed again and again because the Nazi spread of power in Romania and Hungary made the mission too dangerous. Finally the mission received the go-ahead.

Before Senesh left for her training in Cairo, she copied all the poems that she had written in Palestine and entrusted them for safekeeping to her friend Miriam Yitzhaki.

In these and other poems the reader feels Senesh's pain acutely. Senesh describes the conflicts she experiences and the toll of her idealism and heroism. Short and lyrical, her poems speak of longing, meaning,

"I see the hand of destiny in this just as I did at the time of Aliyah [moving to Palestine]. I wasn't master of my fate then either. . . . I was enthralled by one idea, and it gave me no rest. . . . Now I again sense the excitement of something important and vital ahead and the feeling of inevitability connected with a decisive and urgent step."

—Hannah Senesh

Jewish parachutists from Palestine with Yugoslavian partisans in Yugoslavia. Hannah Senesh stands in the top row. (Yad VaShem)

and passion. But they also speak of loneliness and pain.

Senesh desperately missed her mother in Hungary and her brother George who was in France. In "Loneliness" she records her feelings of isolation, her wish to meet someone who will understand her completely, to whom she can tell all.

In "To My Mother," Senesh acknowledges the pain that her departure has caused her mother. The poem describes the sacrifice her mother is making and pays tribute to her. Even a poem celebrating plowing the winter land at Kibbutz Ginosaur (where she temporarily resided) acknowledges that while there is joy in the winter plowing in Palestine, in Europe there is pain.

Senesh sensed that danger was imminent. She could feel the war closing in on her. In her poem "To Die," she proclaims that she does not want to die, that she loves life.

But despite the danger, Senesh's feeling of responsibility for others led her to volunteer to return to war-torn Europe. "It is better to die and free our conscience," she told her comrade Yoel Palgi, "than to return with the knowledge we didn't even try." The poem "Blessed Is the Match," which she wrote in the midst of her dangerous mission, proclaims Senesh's enormous courage.

In this poem Senesh declared her dedication to morality and justice. In her journal, Senesh had written that she "wanted to be a spark of all that was good in the world." In the midst of her struggle, knowing that she might sacrifice her life, she saw herself as that spark.

Soon after writing that poem, Senesh was guided to the Hungarian border by partisans, civilians who banded together to fight the Nazis. It wasn't until June 9, 1944, the same day that the Germans began expelling Jews from most of Hungary's cities, that Senesh crossed over to Hungary. After crossing the border, two of the partisans she had traveled with were stopped by the police. Instead of answering questions, one took out a gun and shot himself, probably out of fear and desperation. Senesh and a companion hid in the woods. But they were soon found by the Hungarian police and taken to prison.

The transmitter she'd hoped to use to send messages to the Allies was found in the bushes. The Hungarian police tortured her, trying to learn the radio code. They beat her for hours until her face was swollen beyond recognition; they knocked out one of her teeth, and they brought her mother to prison in Budapest and threatened to hurt her. Still Senesh would not reveal the code. She would not imperil the Allied war effort.

Even after she was caught and imprisoned, Senesh did not give up. She continued to inspire others. When the sun was in her cell, Senesh used a mirror to flash signals to Yoel Palgi, a fellow paratrooper who had also been imprisoned. After Senesh's mother had been detained for interrogation about Senesh's spy activities, she had also been imprisoned. Senesh could see her mother's window from her own. To speak to her mother, she spelled out letters in the air with her finger.

Later Senesh cut out large letters from scrap paper. She had to stand a chair on top of a desk on top of her bed to hold the letters up to her window. There was the danger of being caught, but Senesh was persistent. She began holding conversations with those prisoners whose windows opened on to hers. She encouraged them, gave them information she learned when she was taken outside the prison for interrogation, and told them of the life she had led in Palestine. Senesh had to communicate; she would not be silent.

After a short trial, Senesh was killed by a firing squad on November 7, 1944. Even the people who had captured, tortured, and killed her could not help but admire her stubborn persistence, her independence, and her refusal to yield. "I must pay tribute to your daughter's exceptional courage and strength of character, both of which she manifested until the very last moment," Judge Simon, the military prosecutor of the case, told Senesh's mother, Catherine.

Nobody knows who buried her in the martyr's section of the Jewish cemetery in Budapest. Three months after Hannah was killed, Budapest was liberated by the Russian army. Although Catherine had survived, 70 percent of Hungarian Jewry had been killed during the war.

In 1950, Hannah's body was exhumed and flown to Israel where she was buried at Mount Herzl in the national military cemetery.

Hannah's diary has been published in at least 13 different editions. In Israel today, there are 32 streets, a ship, a forest, and 2 farming settlements named after Senesh. Her mother and brother moved to Israel, and Senesh has nieces, nephews, and grandnieces living there. In Kibbutz Sdot-Yam, the library is named in her honor. Many of her poems have been set to music. Many schoolchildren still recite the poem "Blessed Is the Match." At the Holocaust Museum in Jerusalem, run by Yad VaShem, the official Israeli institution charged to commemorate the Holocaust, its victims, and heroes, a visitor can see the scrap of paper on which it is written.

Chronology

July 17, 1921	Hannah Senesh born in Budapest
1933	Nazis take control of German government
1934	Senesh begins her diary
September 1, 1939	World War II begins
September 13	Senesh leaves for Palestine
1939–41	studies at Nahalal Training School
1941–43	joins Kibbutz Sdot-Yam
1944	joins paratroopers; leaves for Yugoslavia; writes "Blessed Is the Match"
June 9	crosses Hungarian border
October 28	tried by Hungarian court
November 7, 1944	Hannah Senesh executed
1950	Her body is flown to Israel and buried with full military honors

Further Reading

Hannah Senesh's Works

Hannah Senesh: Her Life and Diary. Translated by Marta Cohn. New York: Schocken Books, 1976. Includes an introduction by Abba Eban, the former Israeli foreign minister. Selected diary entries and poems. Also includes writings about Hannah by her mother, and comrades Yoel Palgi and Reuven Dafne.

Works About Senesh

Atkinson, Linda. *The Story of Hannah Senesh, 1921–1944.* New York: Lothrop, Lee, and Shepherd, 1985. A biography of Hannah Senesh for young adults written with the cooperation of George Senesh, Hannah's brother. Excellent account of Hannah's life.

Hay, Peter. *Ordinary Heroes, Chana Szenes and the Dream of Zion.* New York: G.P. Putnam's Sons, 1986. Written by a friend of the family. Detailed account of Hannah's life.

Masters, Anthony. *The Summer That Bled: The Biography of Hannah Senesh.* London: Michael Joseph, 1972. A biography that focuses on Hannah's life in its historical context.

Schur, Maxine. *Hannah Szenes—A Song of Light.* Philadelphia: Jewish Publication Society, 1986. A concise, illustrated young adult biography. (Hannah Senesh's name is spelled differently because some writers prefer to keep her name in the original Hungarian or Hebrew spellings.)

Whitman, Ruth. *The Testing of Hannah Senesh.* Detroit, Mich.: Wayne State University, 1986. A historical introduction by Livia Rothkirchen contains an excellent, concise overview. Whitman writes a series of compelling first-person narrative poems in the voice of Hannah Senesh.

Ida Fink lived under an assumed identity during the war and later wrote stories and a novel based on her experiences. (Courtesy of Ida Fink)

Ida Fink

(1921–)

Their dog, Ching, saved them. It was 1942 in Zbarazh, Poland. The Fink family hid in a doorless pigsty; they knew the Germans were searching for Jews and brutally shooting them or taking them away on transports. When the Nazis strode up to the house, the Finks' loyal housekeeper, Agata, spoke to the Germans. She told them that she didn't know where the family was. Then an SS officer noticed the dog. "Take us to your master," the German said. The dog did not move. The dog did not give them away. But he did bark and nip at the German. The SS man kicked him brutally.

A year later, when members of the family escaped from the ghetto, the Germans found Agata, the housekeeper, at her brother-in-law's home. She had the dog with her. Angered that they couldn't find the family who had fled the ghetto, the SS demanded a piece of rope. They hung the dog from the branch of a cherry tree, their vengeance for not being able to find the family. Ida Fink was a member of that family, and Ching was her dog.

Fink was born in January 1921 in Zbarazh, Poland. Her mother was a high school teacher, and her father was a doctor. Fink studied piano and music theory at a conservatory, but her studies were interrupted by the outbreak of war.

The Germans invaded Poland on September 1, 1939. Later in the month, the Soviet Union annexed parts of eastern Poland, including Fink's town, Zbarazh. Then in June 1941, the Germans invaded eastern Poland, wresting control from the Soviets and occupying Zbarazh. A ghetto was established in late summer 1942. After the Wannsee Convention in 1942, the annihilation of the Jews became Nazi state policy. Deportations to death camps, Belzec and Treblinka among them, soon followed. But, at the end of 1942 Ida and her sister were able to escape from the ghetto with Aryan identity papers that their father had obtained for them. They lived under false identities for the duration of the war, until 1945.

By the end of the war, 90 percent of Poland's 3.3 million Jews had been killed. Fink, her sister, and their father survived. After the war, Fink married and had a daughter. Although the family wanted to move to Israel, they had no permission to do so. Not until 1957 were Fink and her family able to leave Poland and immigrate to Israel.

In the 1950s, Fink began writing about her experiences during the war. Her first book, *A Scrap of Time,* written in Polish, was first published in English in 1987. The book, a series of stories based on her own experiences or experiences recounted to her by family and friends, won the Anne Frank Prize for literature. Her second book, *The Journey,* is an autobiographical novel about two sisters who survive the war using false Aryan identity papers.

Fink currently lives in Holon, near Tel Aviv. Her third book, a collection of stories called *Traces,* was published in 1997.

A Scrap of Time comprises 22 stories and a play. Most of the stories describe everyday life during the German occupation of Poland. But the ordinary life they depict is far from ordinary—it is twisted. The people are trapped in the ghetto, hiding in pigpens or forests or closets. They are caught in hopeless situations, daily facing horror and death.

The stories are short. The language is spare. The scenes are drawn quickly, and the narrator exits without editorializing or sentimentalizing. The details speak for themselves. The writer tells the stories in a whisper, tenderly. The reader is not confronted with the brutality of the camps but rather with the horror of the choices that people were forced to make.

The title story of *A Scrap of Time* describes the first "action," the first killing of Jews. The Jews of the town are ordered to the marketplace. The narrator sees the marketplace from afar and runs away. Later she hears of the death of her young cousin. He had been in hiding, but something had impelled him to join the rest of the Jews in the marketplace. He threw a note from the truck taking him to his death: "Tell my mother that it is my own fault and that I beg her forgiveness."

As a result of such pain and brutality, time itself seems to lose its meaning. Ordinary time as the people have known it stops. "This time was measured not in months but in a word—we not longer said 'in the beautiful month of May,' but 'after the first "action," or the second, or right before the third.'"

Later the narrator hears how her cousin was executed by the Nazis after being forced to dig his own grave. He was killed climbing a tree, hugging the trunk as if he were hugging his mother. Fink paints an extremely powerful image, filled with the emotions of longing, hope, and pain.

Love itself becomes twisted in these stories: Something that once brought joy now brings pain. The love of a parent and child becomes

"I thought that one should speak about this [the time of the Holocaust] in a quiet voice."

—Ida Fink

an instrument of destruction rather than of salvation. In "A Spring Morning," a father's love for his young daughter leads him to urge her to escape from being led to her execution. But as she does so, she is shot by a German soldier. Her father picks her body up and waits for a second shot, to kill him. But he must carry her: ". . . he understood that they would not kill him here, that he had to keep on walking, carrying his dead child."

In "Splinter," a boy mourns the mother who saved him. He wishes that he had let go of the door handle where he was hiding so that he could have joined her. The price of survival is high. The survivors do not walk away unscathed but burdened.

In "Crazy," a father who didn't try to save his children longs to escape his pain. When his children were being taken away in an action, he saw them on the truck. The youngest one cried out to him. "I put my finger to my lips and shook my head at them, they shouldn't cry out, they should be quiet. Sha." In the story he is crazy, but not crazy enough to forget his suffering. Fink shows how the instinct for survival itself becomes distorted, because survival may include sacrificing others or being saved by loved ones who have martyred themselves. Living has a price. The guilt and pain are immense.

Yet as much as the lives of the Jews are degraded so that life becomes unrecognizable, ordinary life does continue for others. In "The Garden That Floated Away" everyday life continues for the non-Jewish neighbors who share the narrator's garden, even while the narrator and her family are unsure they'll even be around in the winter to eat the apples that grow there. As the neighbors pick the fruit, the narrator's father negotiates identity papers with a woman in his office. The narrator sees the garden float away for a moment. The life she knows is over.

In the story "Pig," the peasants are upset about a pig being run over by a truck carrying Jews to their deaths, yet they do not utter a word about the Jews in the truck. In "Splinter," as a boy tells the story of his mother's death to a girl, she falls asleep. These stories demonstrate that there are those who cannot identify with the pain of others.

Even the beauty of nature becomes warped. In "Jean Christophe," nature continues to be magnificent but silent, even as Jews are being killed by the Nazis.

> The silence was horrifying because we knew that there was shooting going on and people screaming and crying, that it was a slaughterhouse out there. But here there were bluebells, hazelwood, daisies, and other flowers, very pretty, very colorful. That was what was so horrifying—just as horrifying as wondering whom they had taken.

Nature is implacable—unmoved by human suffering.

The final piece in the book is a play entitled *The Table* that takes place 25 years after the war. In it, Jewish victims of an action are being interrogated to try to identify the German who shot the Jews in the marketplace. The burden of proof falls on the Jews. Physical evidence becomes primary. Emotional testimony is discounted. While trying to give details of a selection to prove who was in charge, one witness answers: "Oh you want proof, don't you? The snow on the town's streets was red. Red! Does that satisfy you?" The prosecutor responds: "Unfortunately, Mr. Zachwacki, snow doesn't constitute proof for judges, especially snow that melted twenty five years ago."

But for the witnesses, it does. For the witnesses, that snow is not twenty-five years old. The snow hasn't even melted in their mind. The play exposes the gap between emotion and cold logic, implying that cold logic, the logic that the Nazis employed in their systematic annihilation of the Jews, is insufficient.

Fink's second book, *The Journey* (1992), is a novel about two sisters who survive the war with forged Aryan identity papers that their father obtained for them. The girls pretend to be impoverished non-Jewish Polish workers on their way to Germany to volunteer for work. The book is a tale of their survival and anxiety, their hope and despair. It is also a story of identity. "Well children, take your pick, choose new last names," their father tells them. They need to disguise their Jewish names and their Jewish faces. As they get ready for their journey, they dress in peasant clothes. As the narrator ties a kerchief over her hair, her face changes. "It belonged to a girl I didn't know. . . ."

During their ordeal, with each close call, each narrow escape, the girls take on new names, new stories. They put on identities like clothes, hoping for protection. They live in constant danger and fear. Right from the start, they are hounded by informers who suspect them of being Jewish. Their documents are taken from them and they have to find blackmail money to pay off the informers. One of the sisters is offered a hiding place by an acquaintance, but she refuses because there is no space for her sister. After they arrive in Germany to begin work in a munitions factory, the other girls working in the factory suspect them of being Jewish and subject them to tests: saying the Christian prayers and singing Christmas carols. Anti-Semitic taunts are common. Eventually the other girls inform on them. The narrator describes those girls: "Possibly they weren't evil. But a blind hatred was deeply rooted in all of them, and neither words nor kindness could penetrate that dark jungle of primitive instinct."

When the other girls denounce the sisters, the two girls run away in mortal fear. Their lives are at stake. But help comes from unexpected quarters: from the German commandant of the factory who helps them escape by telling them what time the train leaves.

When they arrive at their next destination, without food or shelter, they are forced to knock on the door of a village house. In order to appear like uneducated peasants, they pretend that they don't know German. They are sent to the police station and then sent to work on two different farms. Although the narrator tells her new employer that she knows how to milk cows and clean windows, she fears her lack of knowledge will give her away.

When the separated girls have to escape, the narrator confesses to a fellow farm worker that she is a Jew. The worker helps her by sending messages to her sister. But her sister is too sick to escape. The other sister waits for her, even though each passing day brings more possibility of being caught.

In the midst of this horrible stress, the sisters preserve their allegiance to each other. They are also helped by others, such as the farmhand who has retained his humanity.

They escape again but are questioned at a train station by a policeman. By this point the narrator has learned to act with confidence. "My husband is at the front," she tells the policeman. "Where did I find that tone: offended but calm, and convinced of being right?"

Later, exhausted and fearful, the girls lack the strength to continue and let themselves be caught. They are taken to a police station. A policeman there tells them he is calling the Gestapo. Yet at that moment, the head of the police walks in the door. The narrator tells us: "Sheer chance, the perfect concurrence of two events. The policeman put down the receiver."

Inexplicably, they are saved and sent to another farm. In spring 1945, the Germans surrender. French soldiers drive into the town.

The girls are reunited with their father. Their identities are restored. In the epilogue, the narrator returns to the police station where they were told that the Gestapo was being called. "Our fate suddenly came to a halt and hung there for a moment, suspended over the abyss it had been racing toward, hung there for a few minutes (five? six?) and then just as suddenly turned. This was why I had come here, just for that moment at the crossroads, that sudden turn, that circus trick performed by our fate."

They survive because of their luck, their will to survive, and their courage. But survival comes with a price: anxiety, fear, and suffering.

Ida Fink (Yad VaShem)

Ida Fink's most recent book of short stories, *Traces*, continues to explore the way that ordinary life coexisted with Nazi brutality. When they can, her characters continue to seek love, to play music, to cook, to sew, even as they live in fear and danger.

The stories are heartbreaking, especially the stories about characters who are trying to uncover after the war traces of what happened to their loved ones. In the title story, a woman searching for her sister after the war finds her sister's initials carved in a windowsill and discovers that her 14-year-old sister might have had a baby. In "An Address," a man searches for his wife and receives a telegram that she is alive. However, he is shattered when the woman turns out not to be his wife, but a stranger, a different woman with the same name.

In the story "Cheerful Zofia," years after the war Zofia is always laughing because she is in shock. After hiding in a barn by herself for over a year during the war, she has forgotten her family, her name, who she was. She says, "Other people suffered so much. . . . But no one beat or tortured me. . . . I never saw a German. . . . But still it's as if they killed me."

Zofia and others like her are the "walking dead." Fink shows us that although people survived, their losses are unendurable. Her voice is an intimate one. This is what life was like then, she tells us. This is what we lost. Fink's work exposes the reader to the anxiety and horror of living in a world on the edge of unimaginable terror.

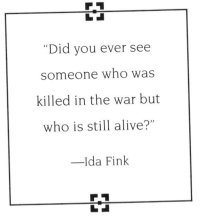

"Did you ever see someone who was killed in the war but who is still alive?"

—Ida Fink

Chronology

January 1921	Ida Fink born in Zbarazh, Poland
1939–42	lives under German occupation and in ghetto
1943–45	in hiding; then works in Germany with false Aryan papers
1957	moves to Israel
1987	publishes *A Scrap of Time* in English translation
1992	publishes *The Journey*
1995	awarded the Yad VaShem Prize, for her writing about the Holocaust
1997	publishes *Traces*

Further Reading

Ida Fink's Works

The Journey. Translated by Joanna Weschler and Francine Prose. New York: Farrar Straus Giroux, 1992. A novel about two sisters who survive the war under false identities.

A Scrap of Time and Other Stories. Translated by Madeline Levine and Francine Prose. Evanston, Ill.: Northwestern University Press, 1995. Stories that portray life in occupied Poland. Also includes a play, *The Table,* about a war-crime interrogation of Jewish survivors.

Traces. Translated by Philip Boehm and Francine Prose. New York: Metropolitan Books, 1997. Stories about life in occupied Poland as well as stories that describe the survivors' search for clues about what happened to loved ones who did not survive the war.

Works About Ida Fink

Furstenberg, Rochelle. "The Ghost Artist" in *Jerusalem Report,* November 27, 1997, pp. 50–51. A short profile of the author and her writings.

Rittner, Carol, and John K. Roth, eds. *Different Voices: Women and the Holocaust.* New York: Paragon House, 1993. This book examines women's experiences during the Holocaust. Includes a short biography of Fink and excerpts from her work.

Arnošt Lustig survived three concentration camps. He has written numerous books of fiction and short stories. (American University)

Arnošt Lustig

(1926–)

He'd already been imprisoned in three different concentration camps. Now in the spring of 1945, 19-year-old Arnošt Lustig was on a train, surrounded by Nazi guards, on his way to almost certain death at Dachau concentration camp. Suddenly, machine-gun fire blasted from the sky. The shooting came from an American plane that was looping and diving overhead, closer and closer to the train. The pilot thought he was aiming at an enemy transport—he was, but this enemy transport carried Nazi prisoners. The plane swooped on its side, hovering over the train, as if it wanted to sever the train in two. Lustig and a friend jumped, knowing it was their only chance for escape—from the machine-gun fire and from the death that awaited them at Dachau.

The young man's escape was successful. Lustig was able to find his way back to Prague, the capital of Czechoslovakia.

Arnošt Lustig was born in Prague in 1926. In 1939, when he was 13, the Germans occupied Czechoslovakia and cut his childhood short. (The country's western provinces of Bohemia and Moravia, including Prague, were occupied and declared a protectorate of the German Reich, or empire.

Slovakia, an eastern Province that had pro-German leaders, was allowed to declare itself an independent state.) Jewish children were not allowed to attend school. Jews could not have radios, bicycles, or even pets. During this period, Lustig became an apprentice tailor and leather worker.

In 1942, he and the rest of the Jews of Prague were expelled to Theresienstadt, an army town where a Jewish ghetto had been established. At first the Jews thought that conditions at Theresienstadt would be favorable. Fifteen separate children's homes were established, where the children lived and studied together. Theater, music, and the arts were also permitted in Theresienstadt; however, the education and cultural activities that were allowed were really a facade in preparation for an expected visit by the Red Cross. In Theresienstadt, people suffered from disease and starvation. The dead lay in the streets. Theresienstadt was actually a way station for Jews headed for the death camps.

Sixteen-year-old Lustig spent his time in Theresienstadt digging track beds for a railroad and air raid shelters for a German hospital. And then he, like most of the rest of the 140,000 Jews who passed through Theresienstadt, was transported to Auschwitz.

Out of 15,000 children who had been in the camp, only 150 survived the war. Less than 10 percent of the Jews of Bohemia and Moravia were alive at the end of World War II.

Lustig survived both the Auschwitz and Buchenwald concentration camps.

After the war, he lived in Czechoslovakia where he studied journalism and worked for Radio Prague. He was sent to Israel as a correspondent in 1948, during the Israeli War of Independence. He later wrote screenplays, novels, and short stories.

In the 1950s and 1960s, Lustig was involved in Czech filmmaking, and played a major role in the Czech new wave cinema movement. Many of his novels were made into films. During this period Lustig was a member of the Communist

Party, because he believed that a Communist society would be a more equal one in which a totalitarian leader like Hitler could not come to power. But he became increasingly disenchanted with Communist restrictions and began to fight for a more liberal society. In 1968, after the Soviets invaded Czechoslovakia, Lustig was forced to leave his country. Soon after, he moved to the United States where he is presently a professor of literature and film at American University in Washington, D.C. He and his wife, Vera, have two children.

Lustig's work is unusual because it is the work of a man who emerged from the Holocaust with faith in people's ability to act ethically. During the war, he saw people who were still able to give and to show concern for others. He witnessed acts of altruism, acts of sacrifice, and acts of love. His work documents those acts of heroism.

Lustig does not claim that ethical acts are easy or simple. His book *Diamonds in the Night* (1962), a collection of short stories, demonstrates the difficulty of behaving ethically during the Holocaust. In "A Bite to Eat," a story that takes place in the Łódź ghetto, a boy's dead father is laid out in the hallway. The boy steals the father's pants, selling them for a piece of bread. He gives the bread to his family, unable, although he is starving, to eat even a bite himself. Later, he yanks out his father's gold tooth, selling it for a lemon to help his sick sister. The story ends with the boy crying. He has given his family the chance for survival, yet he suffers for his actions, knowing that he has desecrated his father's body. Still his actions are diamonds in the night—lights in the darkness, the light of a person acting courageously.

One of Lustig's most important books is *Darkness Casts No Shadow* (1977). The story of two teenage boys (Manny and Danny) who escape from a transport when their train is attacked by an American plane, the book relates the two boys' quest for survival. Told in simple prose with many flashbacks to life in the concentration camps, the novel is powerful and upsetting. It was later made into a movie.

Starving, lost, and in pain, the two boys try to find their way to safety. The book is a grueling account of their hunger and fear. It is also the story of their bond with each other. "He hadn't been so alone any more. Nor ever again. He recalled it now, how he got dysentery and thought he'd never get over it, and how Danny kept on cheering him up and he didn't believe him. To prove his friendship he borrowed Manny's infected spoon to eat his barley and beetroot mess. And so Danny got it too and they lay side by side." They die side by side as well, killed by a German extermination squad: "They faded into the night, like a slim double shadow."

What is important to Lustig is a person's ability to rise above his own need for survival and care for the needs of others, even at the peril of death. For Lustig, the Holocaust showed people at their most depraved but also at their most heroic.

A Prayer for Katerina Horovitzova, is the story of a young girl discovering her own courage. The novel is unusual because it is based on the true story of a group of American Jews who were captured in Italy in 1943 and taken as prisoners by the Nazis. The book is emotionally punishing because it ensnares the reader in a web of Nazi lies and duplicity.

Katerina, a young Polish Jewish woman, is saved from the gas cham-

> "I like people who are fighting for their fate, and who are better in the end, richer, in a sense, than they were in the beginning.
> I think that each writer has a certain duty— to imagine himself in theory as perhaps the last human being alive under certain circumstances and that perhaps his testimony will be the last one."
>
> —Arnošt Lustig

bers by the leader of the group of wealthy American businessmen, Herman Cohen. They meet at the debarking ramp of a death camp in Poland. The American Jews believe that they will be transported to safety because of their nationality. Herman Cohen bribes the Nazi commandant in order to save Katerina, whom Cohen admires because of her youth and beauty. She joins the group of Americans. A train arrives for them, and though they are heavily guarded by Nazi soldiers, the group is assured that the train will take them to a boat that will take them home. But the Nazi commander keeps demanding ransom payments. No matter how much money the men give him, he demands more. The group repeatedly acquiesces, never realizing that the trip itself is a ruse. They will end up at the camp from which they started. Their money cannot protect them. They will share the fate of the rest of the Jews in the camp.

Katerina does finally see the truth of the situation. The group of Americans has been returned to the camps on the pretense of attending a wedding. Told that they need baths before the last leg of the journey, the group is shown into a dressing room. There, Brenske, the Nazi commandant, asks them to undress " . . . we're back on camp territory again. For this reason it is essential—for you and for us—to abide absolutely by all orders, because regulations are sacred here." But Katerina understands that they are to be killed. She grabs a pistol from the lieutenant guarding them and kills him. The group, including Katerina, is killed. But Katerina's act is a just revenge, a moral rectification of evil. Her act of revenge becomes a sacred act—a prayer. The book, a stirring account of a woman's movement from ignorance to heroism, was nominated for a National Book Award in 1974.

One of Lustig's most well-known stories is "Steven and Anne," in the book *Night and Hope*. It tells the story of two young people who manage to find love before they are separated and one is sent to the ghetto and the other to the camps. In *By Words Alone: The Holocaust in Literature*, author Sidra Ezrahi states that in many of Lustig's stories, he carves "islands of adolescent love, loyalty, and moral sanity in the midst of the squalor and misery of the ghetto." The stories in *Night and Hope* show moments of hope in the midst of night, in the midst of despair and atrocity. The ability to love under these desperate conditions becomes an act of heroism.

Lustig shows us that love, courage, and empathy are possible even under the most grueling, nightmarish conditions. A person's task is to identify with others, to connect with others in their pain, and to act ethically even in the most bitter circumstances. Some of Lustig's work is weighted with interior monologues, which he uses to show us that how a person thinks affects that person's behavior. The ability to think empathically, to connect imaginatively to another person, allows a person to behave courageously.

Lustig writes in *Diamonds in the Night*: "Courage in that decisive moment when your life is at stake is also your indifference to that life, and the only yardstick of your courage is the depth of your concern and responsibility for the lives of the others." A person must be ready to die for his or her beliefs. It is not enough just to survive. A person must survive with a clear conscience, with concern for others intact.

Other collections of Lustig's short stories include *Indecent Dreams,* and *Street of Lost Brothers.* Both books address people's struggles with brutality and injustice. Lustig continues to write screenplays, short stories, and novels. He continues to question how people can live moral lives in the face of cruelty. He continues to insist that ethical behavior is not only possible but necessary.

Chronology

1926	Arnošt Lustig born in Prague
1942	sent to Theresienstadt concentration camp; transferred to Auschwitz
spring 1945	escapes from train carrying him to Dachau; returns to Prague
1950s	becomes a screenplay writer and film-maker; part of Czech new wave cinema
1964	publishes *A Prayer for Katerina Horovitzova* in Czech
1968	Soviet occupation of Prague; Lustig leaves Czechoslovakia
1974	*A Prayer for Katerina Horovitzova* nominated for National Book Award
1976	*Darkness Casts No Shadow* and *Night and Hope* published in English
1985	receives Emmy award for outstanding screenplay for the documentary *The Precious Legacy*

Further Reading

Arnošt Lustig's Works

Darkness Casts No Shadow. Evanston, Ill.: Northwestern University Press, 1985. Two teenage boys escape from a death train in 1945.

Diamonds of the Night. Evanston, Ill.: Northwestern University Press, 1986. A collection of semiautobiographical stories.

Dita Saxova. Translated by Jeanne Němcová. New York: Harper and Row, 1979. A 19-year-old survivor of the Holocaust, who is living in a hostel in Prague a few years after the war, tries to reconcile her past with the promise of the future.

Indecent Dreams. Evanston, Ill.: Northwestern University Press, 1990. Three novellas with female protagonists who struggle to affirm themselves in the midst of brutality.

Night and Hope. Translated by George Theiner. Evanston, Ill.: Northwestern University Press, 1985. Seven stories that describe the world of Theresienstadt.

A Prayer for Katerina Horovitzova. New York: Avon Books, 1973. A novel based on a true story. Twenty American Jewish businessmen and a young European Jewish girl are captured by the Nazis. Ultimately, the girl fights back.

Street of Lost Brothers. Evanston, Ill.: Northwestern University Press, 1990. Short stories that explore the inner worlds of victims and perpetrators of Nazi terror.

The Unloved: From the Diary of Perla S. New York: Arbor House, 1985. The testimony of a 17-year-old girl in a Nazi concentration camp who becomes a prostitute in order to survive.

Works About Arnošt Lustig

Ezrachi, Sidra DeKoven. *By Words Alone: The Holocaust in Literature.* Chicago: University of Chicago Press, 1980. Includes a few brief, incisive references to Lustig's work.

Sherwin, Byron L. "The Holocaust Universe of Arnošt Lustig." *Midstream* (August/September 1979), pp. 44–48. A short essay that discusses Lustig's literary philosophy.

——. "What Are the Lessons? Moral Implications of the Holocaust in Holocaust Literature." In *Answer: The Holocaust,* Franklin Littell, Irene Shur, and Claude Forster, Jr., eds. Westchester, Penn.: Sylvan Publishers, 1988. A comparison of the moral philosophies of Lustig, Primo Levi, and Jerzy Kosinski.

Elie Wiesel was a young boy when he was imprisoned in Auschwitz.
He is a prolific writer and a Nobel Prize–winning humanitarian.
(Bryan McBurney)

Elie Wiesel

(1928–)

Elie Wiesel and his father, Shlomo, had already endured unimaginable suffering. In 1944, they'd been deported from their home in the small Transylvanian village of Sighet. They'd been transported to Auschwitz and transferred to the labor camp at Buna. Now it was winter 1945 and the Nazis were fleeing from the advance of the Allies. As they fled, the Nazis forced their prisoners to leave with them, including 16-year-old Wiesel and his father. Made to run more than 40 miles in one day, many of the prisoners died of exhaustion or were shot by the Nazis for stopping. Wiesel and his father continued to run, despite their exhaustion, despite the pain Wiesel felt in his foot, which was wrapped in rags. Only days before, Wiesel had been operated on—without anesthesia—for his severely infected foot. Wiesel wanted to stop, to sink into the soft snow and let his body rest from the pain and weariness, even if rest meant death. But his father would not let him.

At the end of the march, Elie and his father were loaded onto an open freight car, with no room to sit down, crammed in with other starving and dying prisoners. Given no food, the prisoners ate snow from the shoulders of the men standing in front of them. As men died, the Nazis ordered the other prisoners to toss the corpses off the moving train. Of the 120 men who had been in the freight car, only 12 were alive when they reached their destination: the concentration camp of Buchenwald. Wiesel and his father were among the survivors. But Wiesel's father died soon after.

Elie Wiesel was born on September 30, 1928, in the small town of Sighet, which was then in Romania. In 1940, Sighet became part of Hungary, and today it is again part of Romania. Wiesel's parents owned a grocery store. His grandfather was a Hasid, a devout religious man who loved telling stories. From the age of three Eliezer, as he was then called, studied in a Jewish religious school. He loved his studies and fervently believed in God. He believed that with prayer, good deeds, and fasting, he could hasten the arrival of the Messiah. At the age of 12, he wrote his own book about his views of the Bible.

In 1944, anti-Jewish legislation restricted the Jews of Sighet. They could no longer go to the movies or take public transportation. Their shops were closed. Jews who worked for the state were fired. In April 1944, the Nazis established a ghetto in Sighet. The people of Sighet knew nothing about the concentration camps where Jews had already perished.

A month later, all of the Jews of Sighet were deported. They believed the Germans, who told them that they were leaving the ghetto for a labor camp where families would be able to stay together. Instead, after a train trip of many days without water, they were taken to the death camp of Auschwitz. When they got off the train, men and women were separated. Wiesel had no way of knowing that he would never again see his mother or little sister, Tziporah. Most of the people of his town would be killed. In all, about 70 percent of the Jews of Hungary were killed during the Holocaust.

Wiesel was sent to the Buna work camp at Auschwitz with his father. From there they went to Buchenwald concentration camp, where his father soon died of dysentery. Wiesel was transferred to the children's block of Buchenwald. On April 11, 1945, the Nazis fled as American troops liberated Buchenwald.

After the war, a Jewish aid organization sent Wiesel and other children from Buchenwald to France to recuperate. Wiesel stayed in France and studied at the famous university, the Sorbonne. In 1963 he became a U.S. citizen, and in 1969 he married Marion Rose, who was also a Holocaust survivor. She has translated many of his books from French, the language in which he usually writes, into English. They have one son.

Wiesel has written more than 30 books. Most of them are related to the Holocaust. As a man who possessed a great

Buchenwald, Germany. Liberation. Elie Wiesel is the farthest right on the second tier from below. (Yad VaShem)

faith in God and had it severely shattered during the Holocaust, he struggles to hold on to his faith in man, God, and humanity. But he is haunted by the misery and suffering he witnessed, including the heartbreaking death of his parents and sister. His work concerns itself with such questions as How could God could have let such suffering occur? How could men have committed such atrocities? How could others have stood by in silence?

In 1958, Wiesel published his first book *Night*. A masterpiece, it is a memoir of his life during the Holocaust. This slim book is terrifying in its power. The style is spare. Written in the first person, the book records Wiesel's horrifying ordeal of being taken from his home and the subsequent humiliation and degradation of the concentration camp. Most of all the book describes his loss of belief in a meaningful universe. Wiesel has said, "It was not man who died at Auschwitz but the idea of man." The veneer of civilization was broken. What was uncovered was a brute beast in all its power.

The book is an anguished cry from a boy steeped in a faith that cannot sustain him in the face of unbearable atrocity. On his arrival at Auschwitz, 15-year-old Wiesel saw live babies being thrown on a fire. People, knowing they were going to die, began to recite the prayer for the dead. But Wiesel questioned his faith: "For the first time I felt revolt rise up in me. Why should I bless His name? The Eternal, Lord of the Universe, the All-Powerful and Terrible, was silent. What had I to thank him for?"

Wiesel's life turned into a nightmare: "Never shall I forget that night, the first night in camp, which has turned my life into one long night, seven times cursed and seven times sealed." The innocence and joy and faith in God and in the world that he had felt as a child were no longer possible: "I too had become a completely different person. The student of the Talmud, the child that I was, had been consumed in the flames."

The torture Wiesel endured was excruciating. At age 16, he helplessly watched his father die without medical care, food, or water. Wiesel describes how he woke one morning to see another man sleeping in his father's bed. His father was dead. "They must have taken him away before dawn and carried him to the crematory. He may still have been breathing." Wiesel admits to feeling a kind of relief at having his father gone. He had felt so helpless, unable to care for his father or to alleviate his suffering. But the shame he feels about his father's death is unbearable.

Wiesel records the details of the gruesome hanging of a young boy. One of the prisoners asks, "Where is God?" A voice within Wiesel answers: "Here he is—He is hanging here on this gallows." God, himself, is a young boy on the gallows, killed by the atrocity of Auschwitz.

Wiesel closes the book: "From the depths of the mirror, a corpse gazed back at me. The look in his eyes, as they stared into mine, has never left me."

Wiesel's life work is an attempt to resuscitate that corpse and to give meaning back to life. His work is unique because it is the cry of a believer struggling to hold on to his faith. Although he does not doubt that God exists, he questions the justice of that God. His books explore the meaning of suffering and the meaning of life after the Holocaust.

In his second book, *Dawn*, published in English in 1961, an 18-year-old Holocaust survivor named Elisha is recruited to be part

"My goal is always the same: to invoke the past as a shield for the future; to show the invisible world of yesterday and through it, perhaps on it, erect a moral world where just men are not victims and children never starve or run in fear."

—Elie Wiesel

of the Jewish underground in Palestine and fight against the British who were then in control. When Elisha first learns of the Jewish underground activities, he is fascinated by the Jewish fighter who recruits him:

> I saw in him a prince of Jewish history, a legendary messenger sent by fate to awaken my imagination, to tell the people whose past was now their religion: Come come; the future is waiting for you with open arms. From now on you will no longer be humiliated, persecuted, or even pitied.

Finally, it is the Jews who are fighting back, who inspire fear. But then Elisha is called upon to avenge the hanging of a Jewish fighter. He is told to kill a British soldier. When he accepts the job, he can feel the dead—his mother and father, his teachers—judging him. He kills the soldier, but he is changed by the encounter. "The shot had left me deaf and dumb. That's it, I said to myself. It's done. I've killed. I've killed Elisha." He has killed not just the soldier, but part of himself. After he shoots, the night lifts, but the darkness has his face. He is now part of the darkness, no longer innocent. Acting in history as a perpetrator and not a victim also has a price: the loss of traditional morality.

In the novel *The Accident* (1962), the main character is a survivor of the Holocaust struggling for a reason to continue living. He is haunted by the dead, haunted by what he has endured: ". . . man can become a grave for the unburied dead." All he cared for "had been dispersed in smoke." He can no longer live like other people. "Anyone who has seen what they [survivors] have seen cannot be like the others, cannot laugh, love, pray, bargain, suffer, have fun, or forget." Guilt and shame torment him.

While walking in New York City with the woman he loves, he steps out in front of a cab and is knocked down. It is during his healing from the accident, in his encounters with the woman he loves and with friends who care about him that he finds the strength to continue. He learns that "suffering is given to the living not to the dead. . . . It is man's duty to make it cease, not to increase it." It is up to him to choose life.

Both *Legends of Our Time* (1968) and *One Generation After* (1970) are collections of stories and recollections in which Wiesel returns to the stories that obsess him: the destruction of his hometown and of his family, and the need to recreate them, to rescue their memory in prose. In *Legends of Our Time,* Wiesel writes: "But for me writing is a matzeva, an invisible tombstone, erected to the memory of the dead unburied. Each word corresponds to a face, a prayer, the one needing the other so as not to sink into oblivion." Wiesel's haunted words serve as markers for the dead.

Wiesel rescues the characters that the world has forsaken, the characters the world did not believe, the characters the world did not listen to. He brings back to life the characters the world wanted to obliterate.

Hasidic Jews such as Wiesel's grandfather, Jews who stressed a mystical connection to God, were among the first killed in the camps. In *Souls on Fire* (1972), Wiesel brings these communities back to life, telling the stories of their leaders. He tells us,

> In their communities, no beggar ever went hungry on Shabbat. In spite of their poverty, their misery, they asked nothing of others. And were endlessly surprised by and grateful for the smallest expression of warmth, of generosity. . . . Therefore, they could not survive in a society ruled by cold cruelty, a cruelty both impersonal and absurd.

Wiesel often turns to silence as the most appropriate response to the tragedy of the Holocaust. For Wiesel, there is a truth in silence. In Wiesel's novel *The Gates of the Forest,* Gregor, a Jew in hiding during the Holocaust, is saved by pretending to be unable to speak. When he gives up speech, Gregor realizes, "It's in the silence after the storm that God reveals himself to man. God is silence."

> "One meets a hasid in all my novels. And a child. And an old man. And a beggar. And a madman. They are all part of my inner landscape. . . . The enemy wanted to create a society purged of their presence, and I have brought some of them back. The world denied them, repudiated them, so let them live at least within the feverish dream of my characters. It is for them that I write."
>
> —Elie Wiesel

For Wiesel, there is also truth in madness. In his work, it is often the mad who see the world most clearly. In *Night,* the beadle of the synagogue, deported before the rest of the town, returns to tell the people about the murder of the Jews. The people, however, don't believe him and think he is mad. Similarly, a woman on the transport from Sighet to Auschwitz keeps screaming about a vision that she is having: flames shooting into the sky. The people try to silence her, thinking she is crazy. But in the evening, they arrive at Auschwitz. There, they see the shooting flames of the crematoriums. A later novel, *Twilight* (1988), is set in an insane asylum and opens with the epigraph: "The world couldn't exist without madmen."

But neither madness nor silence ultimately suffice. Anguished silence becomes a cry. Wiesel must speak, must try to understand and express that which cannot be understood. Some of Wiesel's books, such as the *Gates of the Forest,* question the role that historical Christian anti-Semitism played in the eruption of anti-Jewish fervor during the Holocaust.

In Wiesel's later works, the children of the survivors continue to speak and to question. Both *The Fifth Son* and *The Forgotten* are books in which the children of survivors return to Europe and confront their fathers' past. In *The Forgotten*, the son says: "I will bear witness in his place; I will speak for him. It is the son's duty not to let his father die." In *The Fifth Son*, the son says: "I carry within me his past and his secret." The sons must tell the story. The work of witnessing, of speaking out, continues.

For Wiesel, witnessing has taken on a worldwide scope. He is our most prominent spokesman on the Holocaust. But Wiesel has become a passionate spokesman for humanity—a peacemaker and activist—concerned about human suffering wherever it occurs. He is a tireless speaker and campaigner who has traveled to Cambodia, South Africa, Russia, and Bosnia in his work against injustice.

In 1986, Wiesel received the Nobel Peace Prize for his work in human rights. In his acceptance speech he said, "I swore never to be silent whenever and wherever human beings endure suffering and humiliation."

Wiesel is an advocate for the oppressed. In his work, he has faithfully remembered the dead. He endeavors to ensure that their memory serve as a reminder of the horrors of which humans are capable so that atrocity be stopped in the world.

By remembering the dead, Wiesel hopes to redeem them, to transform their memory into a blessing.

Chronology

September 30, 1928	Elie Wiesel born in Sighet, Transylvania
1944	Jews expelled from Hungary; Wiesel arrives in Auschwitz; transported to Buna with father
spring 1945	death march to Buchenwald; Wiesel's father dies
April 11	Buchenwald liberated by U.S. Army
1960	Wiesel publishes *Night*
1962	*The Accident* published
1968	*Legends of Our Time* published
1986	Wiesel receives Nobel Peace Prize
1993	serves as main speaker at dedication of U.S. Holocaust Memorial Museum in Washington, D.C.
1995	publishes *Memoirs: All Rivers Run to the Sea*

Further Reading

Elie Wiesel's Works

Essays

From the Kingdom of Memory: Reminiscences. New York: Summit Books, 1990. Essays on friendship, writing, and the power of memory.

Legends of Our Time. Translated by Steven Donadio. New York: Holt, Rinehart and Winston, 1966. Essays, stories, and autobiographical sketches including an account of the author's return to his native town.

One Generation After. Translated by Lily Edeman and Elie Wiesel. New York: Random House, 1970. Twenty-five years after the war, Wiesel speaks out on issues of Jewish concern and questions the meaning of Auschwitz.

Souls on Fire: Portraits and Legends of Hasidic Masters. Northvale, N.J.: Jason Aronson, 1993. Vivid descriptions and stories of Hasidic rabbis.

Memoirs

All Rivers Run to the Sea: Memoirs. New York: Knopf, 1995. The author recounts the people, places, and events that shaped his life as a writer and humanitarian.

Night. Translated by Stella Rodway. New York: Bantam, 1982. The author's account of the Nazi destruction of his native town and of his concentration camp experience while still a teenager. Considered a masterpiece by many.

Nonfiction

The Jews of Silence: A Personal Report on Soviet Jewry. Translated by Neal Kozodoy. New York: Holt, Rinehart, and Winston, 1966. After a visit, the author describes a people discriminated against, yet proud and maintaining their identity.

Novels

The Accident. Translated by Anne Borchardt. New York: Farrar, Straus and Giroux, 1991. A survivor struggles for a reason to live. Only after a terrible accident does he regain the will to continue.

Dawn. New York: Bantam, 1982. A young Holocaust survivor fights against the British in Palestine. His work with the Jewish underground raises many questions about morality.

The Fifth Son. New York: Schocken Books, 1998. The child of Holocaust survivors travels to Europe to confront his father's past.

The Gates of the Forest. New York: Schocken Books, 1995. A young Hungarian Jew escapes to the forest during the Nazi occupation and later joins the Partisans. Jewish tradition merges with Holocaust nightmare.

The Oath. Translated by Marion Wiesel. New York: Random House, 1973. The sole survivor of his town's destruction has sworn himself to silence.

The Town Beyond the Wall. New York: Schocken Books, 1982. A Jew is captured and tortured by the Russians when he returns to his native Hungary after the war.

Works About Elie Wiesel

Abrahamson, Irving, ed. *Against Silence: The Voice and Vision of Elie Wiesel.* New York: Holocaust Library, 1985. A comprehensive collection of speeches and articles by Wiesel, as well as essays on Wiesel.

Lao, Caroline. *Peacemakers.* New York: Dillon Press, 1994. An interesting young adult biography discussing Wiesel's early years as well as his campaign for human rights.

Pariser, Michael. *Elie Wiesel, Bearing Witness.* Brookfield, Conn.: Millbrook Press, 1994. Short biography with pictures for young adults, focusing on Wiesel's life during the war.

Rittner, Carol. *Elie Wiesel: Between Memory and Hope.* New York: New York University, 1990. These scholarly critical essays concentrate on theological topics.

Rosenfeld, Alvin, and Irving Greenberg. *Confronting the Holo-caust: The Impact of Elie Wiesel.* Bloomington: Indiana University Press, 1978. These critical essays by scholars include analysis of the role of silence in Elie Wiesel's work and a personal essay by Wiesel, "Why I Write."

Stern, Ellen Norman. *Elie Wiesel: A Voice for Humanity.* Philadelphia: The Jewish Publication Society, 1996. A biography for young adults that includes information about Wiesel's human rights work.

Anne Frank before she and her family went into hiding, 1940. Amsterdam,
Holland. (copyright AFF/AFS, Anne Frank Stichting)

Anne Frank

(1929–1944)

When 13-year-old Anne Frank heard her father's words, she was shocked. It was the summer of 1942, and they were walking through the narrow streets of Amsterdam. He told her that for the past year, he had been preparing a hiding place for the family. Rather than fall prey to the Nazis who had invaded their country and were deporting the Jews to concentration camps, the family would disappear. And they would not be alone. Another Jewish family, the van Pels, would join them.

Soon after, on Sunday, July 5, 1942, the Frank family received a notice from the SS, the Nazi security police. The notice required 16-year-old Margot, Anne's older sister, to report to the SS.

The next day, July 6, 1942, the Frank family moved into their hiding place. They could not carry their possessions in suitcases because it might reveal that they were going into hiding, and attracting attention to themselves could be fatal. So they walked along the streets, carrying shopping bags and wearing all the clothes they could. Anne wore two vests, three pairs of pants, a dress, a skirt, a jacket, and more. They walked in the pouring rain. They wore yellow stars, the sign used by the Nazis to identify and isolate Jews. They could not drive or take a streetcar because Jews were prohibited from driving or using public transportation.

The address of their hiding place, 263 Prinsengracht, was the building that housed Mr. Frank's business. Without the help of his non-Jewish staff, people such as Miep Gies, a secretary, and her husband Jan; Bep Voskuijl, another secretary; and associates such as Mr. Kugler and Mr. Kleiman, the family could not have survived in hiding. The staff visited them daily, bringing food, supplies, and equally welcome—news of the world.

When on July 6, 1942, Anne entered the hiding place, it was the last time she would see sunshine as a free person. The next time she left the building would be two years later on August 4, 1944, when Anne and the others were arrested and taken away by a Nazi sergeant and Dutch security police. Of the eight people who hid in the building, only one would survive: Otto Frank. But the world would remember Anne. Because for the two years she hid, she kept an intimate diary of her thoughts and feelings. Anne died, but her diary was saved. And through that diary, translated into more than 52 languages, Anne lives on.

Anneliese Frank was born on June 12, 1929, in Frankfurt, Germany, the second daughter of Otto and Edith Frank. Anne's father had been a lieutenant in the German army during World War I. In 1933, after the Nazis came to power in Germany and began to discriminate against Jews, the family decided to immigrate to the Netherlands (also called Holland). Otto Frank started a business producing pectin, an ingredient used for making jam. Later his company also produced spices.

At first, Otto Frank was sure that the family would be safe in the Netherlands and that Germany would honor the Netherlands' neutrality. But on May 10, 1940, Germany invaded the Netherlands. Anti-Jewish restrictions soon followed, slowly limiting the rights of the 140,000 Jews who lived in the country. First, kosher slaughtering of meat was prohibited. Next Jews were forced to register with the Nazis. Later, Jewish property was confiscated, and in 1941, Jews were prohibited from driving, working in the civil service, or even sitting in a public park. Jews had an eight o'clock

Anne Frank as a young girl, 1935 (copyright AFF/AFS, Anne Frank Stichting)

curfew, were not allowed to go to the movies, and could shop only between three and five in the afternoon at restricted shops. In addition, Jewish children could not attend public school. Then in July 1942, the Nazis began deporting Jews to death camps.

On January 20, 1942, Otto Frank filed papers that he hoped would give his family the right to leave the Netherlands. But it was too late. The family was trapped.

Anne Frank's diary begins on June 12, 1942, her 13th birthday, less than a month before going into hiding. Her last entry is on August 1, 1944, three days before she and her family were caught by the Nazis.

In many ways, Frank's concerns in her diary are typical of many teenagers. Most of all, she wants a friend who will understand her. Her first entry in her diary states: "I hope I shall be able to confide in you completely, as I have never been able to do in anyone before, and I hope that you will be a great support and comfort to me." She names her diary Kitty and speaks to her as a confidante.

Frank also wants understanding from her parents. Although she is close to her father, she is alienated from her mother and records her frustration and bitterness at what she feels are her mother's inadequacies.

The other adults in the hiding place, or secret annex as it was called, also annoy Frank. She is quite funny when describing her frustration at

"Who besides me will ever read these letters? From whom but myself shall I get comfort? As I need comforting often, as I frequently feel weak and dissatisfied with myself; my shortcomings are too great. I know this, and every day I try to improve myself, again and again."

—Anne Frank

living in such close quarters with the other family, the Van Daans (the pseudonym she employs in her diary when discussing the van Pels). She writes, September 28, 1942: "Suddenly Mrs. Van Daan says, 'I too, have an unassuming nature, more so than my husband.' Did you ever! This sentence in itself shows quite clearly how thoroughly forward and pushing she is!"

Later the families make room for another Jew, Fritz Pfeffer, a dentist, so he can hide with them. (In the diary, Frank gives him the pseudonym Dussel, or "stupid" in German.) At first, Frank is willing to sacrifice for the man:

> Quite honestly I'm not so keen that a stranger should make use of my things, but one must be prepared to make some sacrifices for a good cause, so I shall make my little offering with a good will. "If we can save somebody, then everything else is of secondary importance," says Daddy and he's absolutely right.

But soon Frank is annoyed by Dussel, as she must share a room with him. When she explains the rules of the annex—no noise, for example, during the day, no flushing toilets, "he asks everything twice over and still doesn't seem to remember." Later, she grows even more exasperated:

> Just as if I didn't hear enough "ssh-ssh" during the day, for making too much noise, my gentleman bedroom companion now repeatedly calls out "ssh-ssh" to me at night too. According to him, I am not even allowed to turn over. I refuse to take the slightest notice of him, and shall go 'ssh-ssh' back at him the next time.

Like many teens, Frank felt misunderstood. She felt that the adults looked at her as a nuisance although they saw her older sister, Margot, as perfect in every way. Eventually, though, Anne does find understanding: from Peter, the van

Pels's son who is two-and-one-half years older than she is. Although early in the diary she says that he is lazy and a bore, after spending many hours talking with him, she falls in love with him: "From early in the morning till late at night, I really do hardly anything else but think of Peter. I sleep with his image before my eyes, dream about him and he is still looking at me when I awake."

On another day, she writes, "I am so longing for a kiss, the kiss that is so long in coming. I wonder if all the time he still regards me as a friend? Am I nothing more?" Finally he does kiss her: "How it came about so suddenly, I don't know, but before we went downstairs he kissed me, through my hair, half on my left cheek, half on my ear; I tore downstairs without looking around, and am simply longing for today."

Their relationship gave her much comfort although she eventually realized that he was not her intellectual equal. "I committed one error in my desire to make a real friendship: I switched over and tried to get at him by developing it into a more intimate relation, whereas I should have explored all other possibilities." She regretted kissing him because she felt that he lacked the capacity to share her innermost thoughts.

But Frank's diary is more than the story of a teenager's ordinary concerns. It is also the intimate story of a girl who lived under extraordinary pressures, yet refused to succumb to despair.

Frank's diary records the development of her character in the face of adversity: horrible fears of being caught by the Nazis, a monotonous diet, and the claustrophobia of being trapped for more than two years with eight people in close quarters.

But she tried to be courageous and make the best of her situation. She devoted herself to reading and studying. She was especially interested in history but also studied short-hand, French, English, and German, geometry, algebra, geography, and the Bible. She also had a keen interest in her family tree, movie stars, and European royal families.

Her mind was always active. She writes: "Laziness may appear attractive, but work gives satisfaction." She viewed each day as an opportunity for self-improvement, and recommended the course of reviewing one's actions each night in order to remedy any character defects.

She faced terrible fears with courage. More than once, the building was robbed, and the families hiding there were terrified that their hiding place was about to be revealed. But Frank refused to succumb to fear.

She was an optimist, not an innocent. She was aware of the horrible suffering being inflicted on the Jews. In November 1942 she wrote: "The Germans ring at every front door to inquire if there are any Jews living in the house. . . . In the evenings when it's dark, I often see rows of good, innocent people accompanied by crying children, walking on and on . . . bullied and knocked about until they almost drop." She knew that she was fortunate to be in hiding.

One night, she heard shooting and was so terrified, she ran into her father's bed. But in the midst of her difficult situation, she was still able to see the beauty in the world. "And in the evening, when I lie in bed and end my prayers with the words, 'I thank you, God, for all that is good

"I don't believe that the big men, the politicians and the capitalists alone are guilty of the war. On, no, the little man is just as keen, otherwise the people of the world would have risen in revolt long ago! There's in people simply an urge to destroy, an urge to kill, to murder and rage, and until all mankind, without exception, undergoes a great change, wars will be waged, everything that has been built up, cultivated, and grown will be destroyed and disfigured, after which mankind will have to begin all over again."

—Anne Frank

and dear and beautiful,' I am filled with joy. Then I think about 'The good' of going into hiding, of my health and with my whole being of the 'dearness' of Peter."

Writing, too, became a lifeline, a means of survival. April 4, 1944, she recorded in her diary: "I want to go on living even after my death! And therefore I am grateful to God for giving me this gift, this possibility of developing myself and of writing, or expressing all that is in me." She dreamed of becoming a journalist or writer someday.

She spent time writing stories while in hiding. Those stories are part of *Tales from the Secret Annex,* a collection of fables, fiction, and essays that was among the writing found in the annex. Many of the stories are tales of fairies, teddy bears, dwarfs, and angels. In one story, the "Guardian Angel," a young girl loses her grandmother and is orphaned, but the grandmother returns as an angel to guide her. Many of the stories follow a similar pattern—innocent tales of loss and return.

Included in the book are moral tales such as the one entitled "Give" that states, "No one has ever become poor from giving." Also included are fantasies such as "Dreams of Movie Stardom," a touching story in which Frank visits a movie star in Hollywood and even works as a model before discovering that Hollywood life is not for her.

But it is Frank's diary that contains her most powerful writing. And that diary took on added significance when on March 29, 1944, Anne heard that diaries would be collected after the war. In a radio broadcast, Bolkestein, a member of the Dutch government in exile, stated that he hoped after the war to collect diaries and letters of peoples' experiences during the war. Anne began editing her diary, revising passages and omitting others, preparing the book to be read by others.

But suddenly in the morning of August 4, 1944, all eight people in the secret annex were arrested by Dutch Nazis and the German police. Kugler and Kleiman, two of Otto Frank's employees, were also arrested and imprisoned but managed to survive the war.

It is not clear whether one of the workers, perhaps a night guard at 263 Prinsengracht, betrayed the families.

The Franks, van Pels, and Friedrich Pfeffer were first taken to a prison in Amsterdam. On August 8, they were sent to Westerbork, a transit camp in northern Holland. On September 3, 1944, they were packed into cattle trucks and sent from Westerbork, the main concentration camp in Holland, to Auschwitz, an extermination center in Poland. Their train was the very last transport to leave from Westerbork. The German war machine had begun succumbing to the Allied advance.

From Auschwitz, some of the eight were transported to other camps. Hermann van Pels died in Auschwitz.

Friedrich Pfeffer died on December 20, 1944, in the Neuengamme concentration camp. Edith Frank died of starvation and exhaustion in Auschwitz on January 6, 1945. It is not known exactly where Mrs. van Pels died, although it was probably a camp in Germany or Czechoslovakia.

Anne and Margot Frank were deported from Auschwitz at the end of October and taken to Bergen-Belsen in Germany. Both contracted typhus and died, Frank a few days after her sister—sometime at the end of February or early March. Frank was 15 years old. Bergen-Belsen was liberated by British troops just a few months later, on April 12, 1945.

Peter van Pels died in Mauthausen on May 5, 1945, three days before the camp was liberated.

Seventy-five percent of Dutch Jews had perished during the war. Otto Frank was the only member of the secret annex to survive the camps. Learning that his wife had died, he returned to Amsterdam and was crushed to learn the tragic news of his daughters' deaths. In Amsterdam, he moved in with Miep and Jan Gies. Soon after, Miep gave him Anne's diary. She'd rescued it immediately after the families in the secret annex had been arrested. Otto Frank later copied and translated into German the essential parts of the diary. He omitted passages in which Anne talked intimately about her sexuality or where she was cruel in her comments about her mother.

In 1947, a small edition of the book was published in German. Soon after, the book was translated and published in France, England, and the United States. In 1955, the diary was adapted for the stage and made into a Broadway play, and in 1957, it was made into a movie. In 1997, another adaption of the play, this one with more Jewish content than the earlier play, was successfully produced on Broadway.

Because various versions of the diary exist, there are some people who doubt its authenticity. The State Forensic Laboratory in the Netherlands, however, positively identified the diary as Anne Frank's. In 1998, controversy erupted over Frank's diary when five of the pages that Otto Frank omitted were discovered.

More people have read Frank's diary than any other document on the Holocaust. As a result, Frank is looked upon as a symbol. But it should be remembered that her diary is actually the document of a girl living in relatively good conditions during most of the war. Frank's words, "I still believe that people are good at heart" are often cited as proof of her faith in humanity. Yet, as historian Dina Porat, a professor at Tel Aviv University points out, Anne wrote those words while in hiding. She had experienced fear and deprivation, but the horrendous brutality of the concentration camps still awaited her. It is doubtful that she would have written those words later, after she was imprisoned in the concentration camps.

"It's an odd idea for someone like me to keep a diary; not only because I have never done so before, but because it seems to me that neither I—nor for that matter anyone else—will be interested in the unbosomings of a thirteen-year-old school girl." Luckily Anne did keep her diary. And the world continues to be captivated by her humor, honesty, and charm.

Chronology

June 12, 1929	Anne Frank born in Frankfurt, Germany
May 10, 1940	Germany invades the Netherlands; anti-Jewish restrictions soon follow
June 12, 1942	Frank begins her diary
July 6	Frank family goes into hiding at 263 Prinsengracht
March 1944	Frank hears a radio broadcast that diaries of war will be collected after the war; begins to revise her diary
August 1	Frank's last entry in diary
August 8	eight members of secret annex sent to Westerbork
end of October	Frank and her sister transported to Bergen-Belsen
late February or early March 1945	Anne Frank and her sister die of typhus
1947	first edition of diary published
1955	diary adapted for Broadway theater
1957	diary made into a movie
1989	full diary, *The Diary of Anne Frank, The Critical Edition,* published in English
1997	a new version of the play *The Diary of Anne Frank* appears on Broadway

Further Reading

Anne Frank's Works

Anne Frank, The Diary of a Young Girl, The Definitive Edition. Edited by Otto Frank and Miriam Pressler. New York: Bantam, 1997. Excerpts from the edited and unedited versions.

The Diary of Anne Frank, The Critical Edition. Edited by David Barnouw and Gerrold Van Der Stroom. Translated by Arnold Pomerans. New York: Doubleday, 1989. Contains the complete diary: the original and edited versions as well as authoritative essays on the history of the Frank family. Addresses the validity of the diary and the story of the family's arrest.

Tales from the Secret Annex. New York: Washington Square Press, 1983. A collection of stories and essays that Anne wrote while in hiding.

Works About Anne Frank

Gold, Alison Leslie. *Memories of Anne Frank: Reflections of a Childhood Friend.* New York: Scholastic Press, 1997. Hannah Gosslar's memories of her childhood friend.

Lindwer, Willy. *The Last Seven Months of Anne Frank.* New York: Random House, 1991. Eyewitness accounts of six Jewish women who recount Anne's ordeal after she wrote the diary—from the day she was taken by the police from the Amsterdam attic to the day she perished in Bergen-Belsen.

Schnabel, Ernst. *Anne Frank: A Portrait in Courage.* New York: Harcourt Brace, 1959. The author reconstructs Anne Frank's life by interviewing witnesses and investigating documents relating to the German occupation of the Netherlands.

Shawn, Karen. *The End of Innocence: Anne Frank and the Holocaust.* New York: Anti-Defamation League, 1989. A curriculum that allows students to understand Anne Frank and the war that the Nazis waged against the Jews.

Stichting, Anne Frank. *Anne Frank in The World*. Amsterdam: self-published, 1985. A photographic history of both the Frank family and historical events between 1929 and 1945.

Tames, Richard. *Anne Frank*. New York: Franklin Watts, 1991. A young adult biography of Frank.

Van Der Rol, Rund, and Rian Verhoeven. *Anne Frank: Beyond the Diary: A Photographic Remembrance*. New York: Puffin Books, 1995. Photos of Frank and her life.

A novelist and short story writer, Aharon Appelfeld escaped from the Nazis at the age of nine. He survived in the Ukrainian countryside for three years. (Courtesy of Aharon Appelfeld)

Aharon Appelfeld

(1932–)

It was summer 1941. Aharon Appelfeld, a young boy, was on summer vacation with his parents, visiting his grandparents. His grandmother and mother were sitting in the garden. Suddenly a gun was fired. The two women lay dead. German and Romanian troops had brutally killed his mother and grandmother.

Appelfeld and his father escaped and hid in a nearby cornfield. They returned to their hometown, Czernowitz, the capital of Bukovina, but the violence continued. German and Romanian troops were rounding up, deporting, and murdering Jews.

Later in 1941, Appelfeld, his father, and the rest of the Jews of their town were expelled to a concentration camp in the region of Trans-Dniestria. The camp was in the Soviet Ukraine, then under German military occupation. There Appelfeld and his father were separated. Although Appelfeld was only nine years old, he escaped from the camp alone. A beloved only child from a well-to-do family, he was now totally on his own. He had to find food, shelter, clothes, and water by himself. He had to live by his wits. And above all, nobody could ever know that he was a Jew.

For three years, until he was 12, Appelfeld wandered the Ukrainian countryside. Because he had blond hair and because in addition to his mother tongue of German, he had learned Ukrainian from the two maids who had worked in his home, he was able to pass as a non-Jewish Ukrainian peasant. Sometimes he worked as a servant for villagers, who were usually poor, ignorant, and abusive. Sometimes he lived in the woods, scavenging for food. These and other experiences of Appelfeld as a young boy during the war form the core material of his life's work in literature.

Aharon Appelfeld was born on February 16, 1932, in Czernowitz, Bukovina. Until World War I, the area had been part of the Austro-Hungarian Empire. After World War I, Bukovina was annexed by Romania. In 1940, the northern part of Bukovina was incorporated into the Soviet Union. Today it is in the Ukraine.

Appelfeld's parents, like many eastern European Jews, were very assimilated, meaning that they were more concerned with fitting in and getting ahead than with focusing on the rich significance of Jewish tradition. They identified more with secular German culture than with Judaism.

In July 1941, northern Bukovina was occupied by the Germans and Romanian collaborators. German and Romanian soldiers proceeded to massacre the Jews. Ghettos were established and Jews were expelled to camps in Trans-Dniestria where they starved, were murdered, or died of disease. By May 1942, about two-thirds of the Jews who had been deported to Trans-Dniestria were dead.

Appelfeld was one of those who survived. In 1944, when the Russian army invaded the Ukraine, 12-year-old Appelfeld was liberated. He joined the Russian army and worked as an aide in the army's field kitchens. Later he made his way to Italy. In 1946, at the age of 14, Appelfeld boarded the ship *Hagana,* which would take him to Palestine (now Israel). In Palestine, Appelfeld was sent to an agricultural school. Then in 1950, he joined the Israeli army and later finished high school and attended college. Soon after, he began to publish poetry. Married and the father of three grown children, he now lives in a suburb of Jerusalem and is a professor of literature at Ben Gurion University. He is the prize-winning author of many novels and collections of short stories and essays.

Appelfeld's books are unique in their dreamlike quality, which conveys the psychological experience of the Holocaust. His books are not concerned with describing the actual events or historical context of the Holocaust. Instead his writings focus on the way the war affected people before, during, and after the Holocaust. The atmosphere of the work is more important than the plot.

Philip Roth, an American writer and critic, has observed that Appelfeld is a "displaced writer of displaced fiction . . . who has made of displacement and disorientation a subject uniquely his own."

A person is displaced when that individual is compelled to leave his or her home and country. Displacement, in Appelfeld's books, is a literal displacement: Because of the Holocaust, the characters have no home, no place to call their own. But in many of his books, the displacement is psychological as well. The characters have been deprived of meaning and wholeness. As a result, they wander through bleak landscapes looking for "home."

Appelfeld has said that he is always writing about his own childhood. Because he lost his parents in the Holocaust, his characters are always searching for a place where they will feel safe and whole. (As an adult in Israel, he was reunited with his father, whom he had assumed to be dead.)

In *Badenheim 1939,* Appelfeld's first book translated into English, the action of the book occurs before the physical displacement, the deportation of the Jews, occurs. In this fablelike book, vacationers at a resort are so preoccupied with their petty daily affairs that they refuse to recognize the impending doom. In Vienna for a festival, the Jewish guests are confronted with inspectors from the sanitation department who force them to register, place barriers at the entrance of the town, sealing them in, and announce that the vacationers are to be transported to Poland. But the vacationers refuse to see the real events unraveling before their eyes. One character is more upset about the spa pool being closed than about being deported to Poland. Others romanticize their destination: "You could sit in an armchair, listen to music, leaf through a journal, and dream of Poland. The remote alien Poland began to seem an idyllic, pastoral place." They suffer a disorientation, a dislocation from reality.

Appelfeld has memories of his own family vacationing in a spa like Badenheim. Most of the guests were Jews who, like his own parents, had little connection with Jewish tradition and culture. But as Appelfeld said in a conversation with Philip Roth: "Fate was already hidden in these people like a mortal illness. They were certain they were no longer Jews, and that what applied to the Jews did not apply to them. That strange assurance made them into blind or half blind creatures." The people had a self-deception that allowed them to deny the reality of what was occurring.

Badenheim 1939 conveys a strong sense of irony and foreboding because although the characters are not aware of the historical circumstances—the rise to power of Hitler and the Nazis—the reader is.

Appelfeld deliberately leaves out historical explanations in many of his books. He says: "The Jewish experience in the Second World War was not historical. We came into contact with archaic mythical forces, a kind of dark subconscious, the meaning of which we did not know, nor do we know it to this day."

Appelfeld explores these dark forces in most of his work. *Tzili, The Story of a Life* is a novel about a young girl who is forced to survive in a brutal world. Tzili is dull witted, does poorly in school, and is neglected by her family. When war breaks out, Tzili's family runs away and leaves her alone. She must scrounge for food in the forests. She literally has no place—no place in her family and no place to live. "The sights of home dissolved in the cool air." But it is her very simplicity that allows her to endure the animal existence she is forced to bear. Unburdened by memory, doubt, or shame, she is able to survive the sense of being displaced from minute to minute, "She learned to walk barefoot, to bathe in the icy water, to tell the edible berries from the poisonous ones, to climb the trees." Later peasants take her as a servant, but she is routinely beaten and abused. When she runs away, she is content ". . . like a lost animal whose neck has been freed from its yoke at last." She survives because she is a child who can accept what comes to her. She does not live in the past or in search of the future.

"The reality of the Holocaust surpassed any imagination. Had I remained true to the facts, no one would have believed me."

—Aharon Appelfeld

"Tzili is really my story, my inner story," Appelfeld has said. Even now, he has a hard time believing the cruel experiences he was forced to undergo as a young child.

Appelfeld believes that children in particular were able to absorb the full horror of the Holocaust:

> . . . in the case of the children who grew up in the Holocaust, life during the Holocaust was something they could understand, for they had absorbed it in their blood. They knew man as a beast of prey, not metaphorically, but as a physical reality with his full stature and clothing, his way of standing and sitting, his way of caressing his own child and of beating a Jewish child.

Children did not deceive themselves. They could not deny the horror they experienced; they did not deny human beings' capacity for cruelty.

In Appelfeld's next novel, *Land of the Cattails,* a woman desperately searches for her home and a return to an idealized past that no longer exists. It is the summer of 1938, and a Jewish woman, Toni, and her grown son Rudi are journeying back to the remote Ruthenian countryside where she was born. Toni had left the home of her parents and married Rudi's father, a non-Jew who was a drunk and a wife beater. Now years later, she and her son are returning home. "Isn't it wonderful to return home?" Toni asks her son. She has idealized memories of home: "In that vast region there is a little village full of light, and its name is Dratscincz, and there his grandfather and grandmother dwell." The woman is taking her son to look for a sense of place, an innocent past. "His mother had preached to him about the secret existence of this distant place, like a lost object that had to be restored."

But the closer she and her son get to the village, the more menacing is the threat of violence. Toni and Rudi stay in an inn where the Jewish owner has been brutally murdered. Toni's nostalgia becomes tempered by reality. She tells Rudi: "I will conceal it no longer. In this region, Jews are not particularly well liked." Her son gets drunk when they are almost to the village. Toni is unable to rouse Rudi, and she continues on her own. But when Rudi wakes and follows his mother, he finds that she has been taken away. He keeps searching for her and at the end of the book is at a railroad station with other Jews, all of them tragically unaware of their destination. Rudi is unable to reach his mother's home. Instead he is, most probably, traveling toward his death.

For Every Sin is also the story of someone on his way home. Theo, a refugee, is struggling to find his way home after the war. After having been imprisoned in a camp, Theo is still deceiving himself, believing he will be able to return home to the life he knew before the war. He seeks to escape the other refugees who are also on their way home; he wants to distance himself from them. But he is unable to do so. Instead he is confronted with a series of troubling encounters.

Finally Theo realizes that he will never be able to return home: "From now on he would advance with the refugees. That language [German] which his mother had inculcated in him with such love would be lost forever. If he spoke, he would speak only in the language of the camps."

Theo finally understands that he has to identify with loss, with dislocation and abandonment, and with the Jewish people. There is no possibility of returning home, no return to a place of innocence and purity, no return to his mother who has perished in the camps.

Katerina, published in English in 1992, also has a main character searching for a home, a place to feel safe. But in this book, the main character is a non-Jew who has found her sense of belonging with the Jews. Raised by a drunken father and a mother who beat her, Katerina runs away and becomes a wanderer, like many of the Jewish characters in Appelfeld's works. After finding work as a housemaid for Jewish families, Katerina slowly begins to admire the Jews. But as she identifies with the Jews, her life is filled with loss: She gives up a baby she has conceived out of wedlock. Then her Jewish employers are brutally murdered in anti-Semitic pogroms. Katerina is left with their two Jewish children whom she loves and cares for. But they are taken from her. Another of her own children, a baby son, born of a Jewish father, is cruelly murdered, smashed against a wall. Katerina is sent to jail for killing the murderer.

Although she does eventually return home once she is released from jail, she is entirely alone. All the Jews have been taken away, and all that is left are the ruins of their homes: "I knew that there were no more Jews left in the world, and only within me had they found refuge for a moment." But now that she is home, she is the outsider. Boys stand on the hilltops and shout "There she is, the monster."

Nevertheless, although she is alone, she is home and is able to comfort herself with nature: "Now I know that light is what drew me back. Such purity, oh Lord! Sometimes I wish to stretch out my hand and touch the breezes that meet me on my way, because in this season they are soft as silk." Although she is old and infirm, disconnected from both her own people and her beloved Jews, she achieves a mystical state of oneness: "As long as the window is open and my eyes are awake, loneliness doesn't grieve my soul." She has found a kind of peace.

In his books, Appelfeld focuses on the individual, emphasizing each individual's suffering. Appelfeld has made it his mission to "rescue the suffering from huge numbers, from dreadful anonymity, and to restore the person's given and family name, to give the tortured person back his human form, which was snatched away from him." He believes that literature is the best vehicle for allowing readers to enter the world of the Holocaust. Yet he does not confront his readers with brutality. In his books, the horror hovers in the background.

"All true art tirelessly teaches that the whole world rests upon the individual."

—Aharon Appelfeld

Appelfeld succeeds brilliantly. He allows the reader to identify with characters who have suffered and lost. They will never be free of the psychological horror of the Holocaust. When they survive, they will always be searching for a place where they belong, a place where they can feel safe and loved. And in spite of their suffering, these characters endure and retain their humanity.

Chronology

February 16, 1932	Aharon Appelfeld born in Bukovina
1941	Romanian army deports Jews; Appelfeld and his father expelled to Trans-Dniestria death camp
1941–44	Appelfeld escapes and wanders through the Ukrainian countryside
1944–46	works for Russian army; travels through Italy
1946	moves to Palestine
1950	drafted in Israeli army
1950s	studies at Hebrew University; publishes poetry in an Israeli journal
1962	publishes his first collection of short stories, *Smoke,* in Hebrew
1980	*Badenheim 1939* published in English
1983	English translation of *Tzili* published
1987	Appelfeld receives Harold Ribelow Prize for literary excellence
1992	English translation of *Katerina* published

Further Reading

Aharon Appelfeld's Works

The Age of Wonders. Translated by Dalya Bilu. Boston: David Godine, 1981. A novel in the voice of a 13-year-old Jewish boy about the destruction of his family's secure life in his Austrian hometown.

Badenheim 1939. Translated by Dalya Bilu. Cambridge, Mass.: Godine, 1980. In this novel set in the summer of 1939, vacationers at a spa are oblivious to the doom that awaits them.

Beyond Despair: Three Lectures and a Conversation with Philip Roth. Translated by Jeffrey Green. New York: Fromm International, 1994. Appelfeld discusses memory, the role of art, and religious faith in connection with the Holocaust. Brilliant insights and analysis.

For Every Sin. Translated by Jeffrey Green. New York: Vintage, 1990. In this novel set after the war, a young survivor tries to return home, determined to distance himself from the other refugees.

The Immortal Bartfuss. Translated by Jeffrey Green. New York: Weidenfeld, Nicolson, 1988. A portrait of a troubled survivor living in Israel many years after the Holocaust.

Katerina. Translated by Jeffrey Green. New York: W.W. Norton, 1994. A novel about a simple, non-Jewish housekeeper who finds her sense of belonging with the Jewish people.

To the Land of the Cattails. Translated by Jeffrey Green. New York: Grove Atlantic, 1994. A novel about a Jewish woman and her son who journey back to the remote Ruthenian countryside where she was born, trying, unsuccessfully, to reach her home.

Tzili, The Story of a Life. Translated by Dalya Bilu. New York: Grove Atlantic, 1996. A novel about a poor, simple Jewish girl who manages to survive the Holocaust in the Polish countryside.

Works About Aharon Appelfeld

Ramras-Rauch, Gila. *Aharon Appelfeld, The Holocaust and Beyond*. Bloomington: Indiana University Press, 1994. This superb literary analysis of Appelfeld's work includes biographical information.

Novelist Jerzy Kosinski was a young boy in hiding with his family during the Holocaust. (Reproduction by Bryan McBurney)

Jerzy Kosinski

(1933–1991)

Jerzy Kosinski claimed that as a six-year-old Jewish boy in Poland in 1939, he was separated from his parents during the Holocaust. He was forced to wander in the Polish countryside. Trying to disguise himself as a non-Jew, he stayed with different peasants who beat him and brutalized him. One day, hoping that prayer could save him, he took part in a Roman Catholic prayer service. But he dropped the missal, the book of prayers and rites of the Mass. Angry peasants threatened his life, throwing him into a pit of manure. As a result, Kosinski became mute. Not until a skiing accident, many years later, did Kosinski recover his ability to speak.

That was Kosinski's story. He told it in the novel that made him famous, *The Painted Bird*, and he told it to interviewers, claiming it to be his life story. But according to biographer James Park Sloan, Kosinski's life history was not as Kosinski claimed.

It was true that during the Holocaust, Kosinski had lived in the Polish countryside, but he had not been alone. He had been with his parents. His father had found a place for the family in a small village and there, the family pretended to be non-Jews. As for the brutal events Kosinski describes in *The Painted Bird*, they were not literally true.

Jerzy Kosinski was born on June 14, 1933, in Łódź, Poland. His mother was a pianist. Though Kosinski told many interviewers that his father was a professor of languages, the truth was that he was in the textile business. In 1939, when World War II broke out, Kosinski's family moved from Łódź to Sandomierz, a small town in eastern Poland. When in 1942, a ghetto was established in the town and Jews were evacuated to Auschwitz, the Kosinski family moved farther east to the small village of Dabrowa Rzeczycka. There the Kosinskis continued to pretend that they were not Jewish. But the toll was high on Jerzy, who spent his youth forced to disguise his true identity. He lived in mortal fear of being caught. He could not play with the village boys for fear that they would discover his secret.

In 1944, the final 80,000 Jews living in the Łódź ghetto were sent to Auschwitz. All of the Kosinskis' relatives were

A Nazi train on its way to Poland. The inscription on the railcar reads, "We are going to Poland to strike the Jews." (Yad VaShem)

killed. Kosinski and his immediate family survived the war and returned to Łódź in 1947.

Kosinski later studied history and political science in Poland and then at Lomonosov University in Russia before immigrating to the United States on December 20, 1957. His first published work was a nonfiction book based on his travels in Russia. Soon after, as a poor graduate student, he met a rich widow, Mary Weir, whom he later married.

In 1965, he published *The Painted Bird,* a book of fiction about his experiences during World War II. He published many other fictitious works including, *Steps* and *Being There,* but *The Painted Bird* is the only one of his writings that focuses exclusively on his wartime experiences.

Kosinski has been accused of sensationalizing the Holocaust, painting a picture in *The Painted Bird* that is even more monstrous than the actual atrocities that occurred. Others argue that Kosinski didn't even write his own work.

It is true that Kosinski had help with translation, as he wrote in English, which was not his native language. And it is also true that his story is exaggerated.

The book cannot be read as a documentary of the Holocaust. Rather it is a writer's reaction to his experiences. Kosinski himself has said that "As an actor playing Hamlet is neither Hamlet nor merely an actor, but, rather an actor as Hamlet, so is a fictive event neither an actual event nor totally a created fiction with no base in experience; it is an event as fiction." In other words, the book is part reality, and part imaginary.

As a novel, the book has literary merit. *The Painted Bird* describes the bestiality and atrocity of the Holocaust in the most brutal immediate detail. The book explores the dark side of humankind and its capacity for evil. It suggests that survival in such a world demands that a person learn to behave like an animal and that all a person can hope for is to be able to exact revenge from those who mistreat him or her. There is very little hope in the book. The world is exposed as a place of monstrosity. In fact, the book is so scathing in its attack on Polish peasants that it was banned in Poland when it was first published.

There is almost no dialogue in the book. The reader is in a universe where the boy reacts and acts without any real communication between him and others. As the critic Lawrence Langer notes, the boy can gather impressions but is unable to express himself. The boy, himself, is unnamed. Nobody is close enough to him to call him by name.

The reader is forced to encounter the horror of the Holocaust in incident after incident of unremitting terror. The reader himself feels disturbed and assaulted. He enters a world where terror and violence are the norm.

"I am not interested in explicit memory because I do not trust it. In my case memory is always clouded by my desire for inventiveness. I am no camera. I write because this is what makes me want to live."

—Jerzy Kosinski

The book can be read as a bildungsroman, a novel about the education—moral and psychological—of the main character. But in *The Painted Bird* the young boy is *mis*educated. The narrator learns not about facing life with dignity but how to face life as an animal; survival is the only goal. Society and culture offer no shelter, no protection.

The novel begins in 1939 at the start of World War II. A boy, either a Gypsy or a Jew, wanders through eastern Europe. His parents have sent him to be sheltered by a woman in a village, but she soon dies. His protector gone, the boy travels through the countryside, trying to survive.

He is dark-skinned and dark-eyed, different from the blond, blue-eyed peasants. In addition, he doesn't speak their language.

He has one confrontation after another. Each incident is a brutal encounter with an elemental primitive horror. From each experience he tries to unravel the meaning of life in a horrifying universe. Each time the boy thinks he has found the key to understanding the world, he soon learns that the explanation is insufficient.

The boy first encounters people whose belief system is anchored in magic and superstition: primitive belief. In this world, things happen because of evil spirits, and it is a person's task to learn how to avoid evil spirits. Marta, an ignorant peasant, tells him that people with black eyes such as his bring illness. "That is why she forbade me to look directly into her eyes or even those of the household animals." When the bread does not rise, she accuses the boy of casting a spell.

After she dies, he lives with Olga, a healer. She tells him that in eyes such as his, bewitched black eyes, an evil spirit resides. When he falls ill, she plants his whole body in a field. Only his head sticks out, "Like an abandoned head of cabbage." A swarming flock of ravens attack him. Later Olga digs him out.

Perhaps no incident is more sickening than when the boy stays with a miller who has a young plowboy working for him. The miller thinks the plowboy is lusting after his wife and in an act of unparalleled cruelty, he gouges out the boy's eyes with a spoon. "The eye sprang out of his face like a yolk from a broken egg and rolled down the miller's hand onto the floor."

As a result, the protagonist doubts one of the most basic assumptions about life: the integrity of the body. The security of having eyes to see with—of having vision—is violated. "When one bent down they [the eyes] hung like apples from a tree and could easily drop out." The young boy is exposed to human vulnerability and cruelty.

While staying with Lekh, a birdcatcher, the wandering boy receives another negative life lesson. The birdcatcher paints a raven red, green, and blue and then releases the painted bird when a flock of ravens flies over the house. The ravens attack the painted bird, which falls to the ground. "Its eyes had been pecked out, and fresh blood streamed over its painted feathers."

The one who does not fit in is not only maimed but blinded. And the blinding of the "misfit" is carried out not just by man but also by nature. Nature itself is cruel. Revenge is built into the universe. The boy is like the painted bird, trying to fit in but unable to do so, continually terrorized.

The boy next stays with a carpenter. When the man tries to drown him, the boy is able to trick him and lead him to a bunker where the carpenter is eaten alive by rats. The boy has learned to survive.

"Then a new kind of train appeared on the line. Living people were jammed in locked cattle cars. . . . These trains carried Jews and Gypsies, who had been captured and sentenced to death. In each car there were two hundred of them stacked like cornstalks, arms raised to take up less space."

The boy accepts the peasants' beliefs, that the Jews are being punished for killing Christ: "They were

> "Perhaps the best proof that I was not overstating the brutality and cruelty that characterized the war years in Eastern Europe is the fact that some of my old school friends, who had succeeded in obtaining contraband copies of *The Painted Bird*, wrote that the novel was a pastoral tale compared with the experiences so many of them and their relatives had endured during the war."
>
> —Jerzy Kosinski

being justly punished for the shameful crimes of their ancestors, for refuting the only True Faith, for mercilessly killing Christian babies and drinking their blood."

The boy turns to Christianity, to prayer, as a key to the problem of understanding the universe. "I understood why some people were strong and others weak, some free and others enslaved, some rich and others poor, some well and others sick. . . . One had only to recite prayers, concentrating on the ones carrying the greatest number of days of indulgence." But then the priest himself dies. And when the boy takes part in a Christian mass and is asked to carry the missal, he falls backward. The peasants attack him. The trauma of the event causes the boy to lose his voice.

He next turns to love as a force that can save him. He falls in love with a peasant girl, but she betrays him. The belief in love, in prayer, or in magic as governing principles of the world—none has helped him. The boy looks toward evil: "Now I would join those who were helped by the Evil Ones. . . . In time I could become as prominent as any of the leading Germans."

Even at the end of the war, when the boy is saved by the Russian army, the soldiers offer him different principles for living. One argues for the importance of collective life; the second for self-reliance and the ethic of revenge. The boy accepts the ethic of revenge, believing that each man has "his own justice, which is his alone to administer."

The boy's "miseducation" is complete. His experiences have taught him to be barbaric, incapable of being part of a family. Each man is for himself, only.

Even when he is reunited with his parents, "I could not readily accept the idea of suddenly becoming someone's real son, of being caressed and cared for, of having to obey people." In fact, he takes revenge against a stranger, dropping bricks on the head of a movie theater attendant who has humiliated him.

At the end of the book, the boy takes up skiing in order to regain his health. After a serious skiing accident, he regains his speech. But the value of communication is in doubt: "It mattered little if one was mute: people did not understand one another anyway." Communication is impossible.

In Kosinski's world, humans are exposed as alienated monsters, unable to communicate, love, or value life. The vision is bleak. The boy can speak, but what form can speech take now, in the aftermath of the Holocaust, in the aftermath of what is now known of people's abilities to be cruel and bestial?

In his notes to the book, Kosinski says that the peasants were no worse than the city people, educated western Europeans who carried out the mass extermination. Kosinski shocks us with brutality, forcing us to encounter sheer horror at every turn. But it is not the terror of the unknown or of evil spirits. It is the terror of man's capacity for evil.

Kosinski may not be telling the truth. But he is telling *his* truth, one shaped by encountering evil at a young age. Though he survived, he was hurt, maimed. It seems that Kosinski saw himself as a painted bird, one more creative and beautiful than the others, one forced to suffer.

The Painted Bird has enjoyed tremendous popularity and was once required reading in many college and high school classes.

Kosinski had a successful career as a writer, publishing many best-selling books including *Steps* (1968) and *Being There* (1971), both of which explore the issue of identity. *Being There* was later made into an award-winning movie; Kosinski wrote the screenplay.

He won many awards including the National Book Award and a Guggenheim Fellowship. Kosinski was a professor at Princeton University (1969–70) and at Yale University (1970–73). He was also a skier, a photographer, a polo player, and a world traveler. He was even an actor, performing in Warren Beatty's movie *Reds*.

Yet Kosinski never felt at peace with himself. He was devastated by an article that appeared in the *Village Voice* newspaper on June 22, 1982, accusing him of plagiarism. Despite his success, Kosinski was a vulnerable, insecure person, constantly trying to prove himself. Kosinski killed himself in his bathroom on May 3, 1991, while his second wife, Katherine (Kiki), slept in the next room.

Chronology

June 14, 1933	Jerzy Kosinski born in Łódź, Poland
1939–45	Germany invades Poland; Kosinski and his parents hide in two small Polish villages
1947	Kosinski family returns to Łódź
1950	Kosinski graduates high school
1955	completes second master's degree in history
1957	travels to America as Ford Foundation fellow
1965	publishes The Painted Bird
1968	publishes Steps
1969–70	serves as professor at Princeton
1970–73	serves as professor at Yale
1971	writes Being There
1981	acts in Reds
May 3, 1991	Jerzy Kosinski commits suicide

Further Reading

Jerzy Kosinski's Work

The Painted Bird. 2d ed. New York: Random House, 1983. In this novel, a young boy abandoned by his parents in eastern Europe during World War II experiences a series of brutal encounters.

Works About Jerzy Kosinski

Langer, Lawrence. *The Holocaust and the Literary Imagination.* New Haven, Conn.: Yale University Press, 1977. Contains a chapter, "Men into Beasts," that discusses *The Painted Bird* as a novel of atrocity. Insightful literary criticism.

Lavers, Norman. *Jerzy Kosinski.* Boston: Twayne Publishers, 1982. Some of the biographical information is subject to dispute. Shows Kosinski to be an original, brilliant novelist.

Sloan, James Park. *Jerzy Kosinski: A Biography.* New York: Dutton, 1996. Excellent detailed biography that reveals the true life story of Kosinski.

Index

This index is designed as an aid to access the narrative text and special features. Page numbers in **boldface** indicate key topics. Page numbers in *italics* indicate illustrations or captions. A *c* following the page number indicates chronology. An *m* indicates a map.